African Spirituality

Unlocking the Power of Orishas, Yoruba, Santeria, Voodoo, and Hoodoo

© **Copyright 2023 - All rights reserved.**

The content contained within this book may not be reproduced, duplicated, or transmitted without direct written permission from the author or the publisher.

Under no circumstances will any blame or legal responsibility be held against the publisher, or author, for any damages, reparation, or monetary loss due to the information contained within this book, either directly or indirectly.

Legal Notice:

This book is copyright protected. It is only for personal use. You cannot amend, distribute, sell, use, quote, or paraphrase any part, or the content within this book, without the consent of the author or publisher.

Disclaimer Notice:

Please note the information contained within this document is for educational and entertainment purposes only. All effort has been executed to present accurate, up-to-date, reliable, and complete information. No warranties of any kind are declared or implied. Readers acknowledge that the author is not engaging in the rendering of legal, financial, medical, or professional advice. The content within this book has been derived from various sources. Please consult a licensed professional before attempting any techniques outlined in this book.

By reading this document, the reader agrees that under no circumstances is the author responsible for any losses, direct or indirect, that are incurred as a result of the use of the information contained within this document, including, but not limited to, errors, omissions, or inaccuracies.

Free Bonus from Silvia Hill available for limited time

Hi Spirituality Lovers!

My name is Silvia Hill, and first off, I want to THANK YOU for reading my book.

Now you have a chance to join my exclusive spirituality email list so you can get the ebooks below for free as well as the potential to get more spirituality ebooks for free! Simply click the link below to join.

P.S. Remember that it's 100% free to join the list.

~~$27~~ FREE BONUSES

- 9 Types of Spirit Guides and How to Connect to Them
- How to Develop Your Intuition: 7 Secrets for Psychic Development and Tarot Reading
- Tarot Reading Secrets for Love, Career, and General Messages

Access your free bonuses here
https://livetolearn.lpages.co/african-spirituality-paperback/

Table of Contents

INTRODUCTION 1
CHAPTER 1: AFRICAN SPIRITUALITY BASICS 3
CHAPTER 2: OLODUMARE, THE SUPREME GOD 12
CHAPTER 3: WHO ARE THE ORISHAS? 20
CHAPTER 4: THE WHITE ORISHAS 30
CHAPTER 5: THE RED AND BLACK ORISHAS 39
CHAPTER 6: THE ORISHA AND ANCESTOR ALTAR SETUP 49
CHAPTER 7: AFRICAN MAGICAL PRACTICES 57
CHAPTER 8: GRIS, MOJO BAGS, AND VOODOO DOLLS 68
CHAPTER 9: SACRED RITUALS, SPELLS, AND BATHS 78
CHAPTER 10: DAILY PRACTICES WITH THE YORUBA CALENDAR 88
EXTRA: ORISHA GLOSSARY 96
CONCLUSION 101
HERE'S ANOTHER BOOK BY SILVIA HILL THAT YOU MIGHT LIKE 103
FREE BONUS FROM SILVIA HILL AVAILABLE FOR LIMITED TIME 104
REFERENCES 105

Introduction

African spirituality isn't just a fascinating topic filled with interesting mythology, magical rituals, and spells. Learning about it can help you better understand your heritage and culture's rich history. In this book, you'll discover the interesting and ancient world of African spirituality and have all your burning questions answered. The first thing covered is the diversity in African spirituality, its history, and its origins leading to various practices within African spirituality. Learning about them and their historical background can give you a clear idea of African religions, beliefs, and traditions.

Every religion and faith is usually defined by its deities, and African spirituality is no different. Although all their deities play prominent roles, none is more significant than their supreme god. You will not only learn everything about this chief deity, but you'll also discover why he is highly revered in all practices.

If you are familiar with African spirituality, you have probably heard the term "Orishas" a couple of times. These beings play an influential role in African spirituality and all its related practices. In this book, you'll step into the vast and rich world of the Orishas. You'll learn who they are, where they come from, their characteristics, and how they can help you. The book will cover in detail everything you want to know about the Orishas and more.

You can't learn about deities and supreme beings without learning how you can honor them. In this book, you'll learn how to create your own private altar to honor your ancestors and the Orishas. If you are new to the world of altars, don't fret. The book will provide you with step-by-step instructions on how to set up an altar of your own.

Magic and rituals are an intrinsic part of African spirituality. For some people, this may be the most interesting section of the book, and you will not be disappointed. The book will first introduce you to some magical practices, including the well-known Voodoo doll. In the last part of the book, you'll apply everything you have learned to practice various spells, rituals, and baths.

African spirituality isn't just an interesting topic you can read about in your free time. It can become a way of life easily integrated into your daily lifestyle. The book will give you helpful tips so that African spiritual practices easily become a part of your daily routine.

This book will act as a helpful guide, especially if you are a beginner. We made sure to make it as simple as possible to avoid confusing the reader. Although the book is extremely informative, you will not feel overwhelmed by the information provided as it's all presented in an interesting manner. You won't need to look elsewhere as this book includes everything you need to get started, including various methods and helpful instructions.

Prepare yourself for an enchanting journey into the world of African spirituality. This page-turner will be a handbook you'll return to whenever you need help or have a question.

Chapter 1: African Spirituality Basics

Before religions like Islam and Christianity arrived in Africa, the African people had their own beliefs, ceremonies, practices, and festivals, which they referred to as African spirituality. African spirituality, naturally enough, originated in Africa and is derived from the continent's ethnic identity. Each religion that has branched out from the spirituality of Africa is linked to its country's culture and history. For instance, the Zulu religion is based in southern Africa, and the Yoruba religion originated in southwestern Nigeria.

African spirituality originated in Africa and is derived from the continent's ethnic identity.
https://www.pexels.com/photo/a-man-in-maroon-robe-holding-a-burning-stick-8243596/

African religions are incorporated into the people's daily lives because, in African spirituality, all beliefs and practices impact every area of the people's lives. There is a belief that African spirituality is holistic, and spiritualists view certain parts of people's lives differently. For instance, if someone gets sick, they don't consider it simply an ailment of the body. They believe there may be an imbalance in other aspects of the person's life that makes them sick. Taking a holistic approach, questions are asked about the state of family relationships or their relationship with one or more of their ancestors. In fact, the ancestors play a significant role in African spirituality by giving advice to the living, honoring them, and bestowing good fortune on them. However, these gifts come with a price, although it isn't a high one. Sometimes the ancestors make simple demands, like regular maintenance of their shrines.

This begs the question, are these ancestors considered gods? African spirituality is different from other religions because there isn't a fixed concept of a deity. The role ancestors play in the African people's lives differs from one group to another. Some people hold their ancestors in similar regard to deities, while others don't share the same belief. Either way, the African people revered their ancestors. They see them as something more or higher than regular human beings who have the power to bless or curse them.

The ideas of polytheism and monotheism don't exactly exist in African spirituality, as this type of thinking may seem a bit simplistic when describing such a complex belief. Spiritual beings, deities, and gods exist in the world of African spirituality. This makes it difficult to put this belief into one single category. However, some African spiritual beliefs believe in the concept of a supreme being. For instance, the Yoruba believe in a supreme god called Olorun or Olodumare. They believed that Olorun created the universe with the help of other deities called the Orishas. Orishas receive prayers from the people and deliver them to the supreme deity. They help him with other earthly functions as well.

African spirituality is built on the belief that the spirit of the Creator is in everything, including living beings and everything that exists in nature.

Certain elements define African spirituality:
- The Spirit of Being
- The nature of existence
- Cyclical existence
- The interconnectedness of things
- Order and balance
- Social and spiritual hierarchy

African spirituality is diverse. Over the years, various religions have passed through Africa, mainly Christianity and Islam, which changed and impacted the region's culture and did allow African spirituality to evolve throughout time. Over the years, contact with other countries and cultures from all over the world has helped African spirituality grow, and it has been able to adapt to these changes. African spirituality didn't dismiss these religions' beliefs or wisdom. On the contrary, it allowed itself to expand by incorporating their views and wisdom. For instance, you may find verses from the Bible or the Quran on African amulets. On the other hand, these religions resist accommodating African beliefs.

Like other ancient cultures, African spirituality was passed down through oral methods like songs or stories. Therefore, their beliefs weren't collected in a single religious text like the Bible. This made it easier for African spirituality to be influenced by other religions and beliefs. This kind of adaptability is how African spirituality manages to deal with modernity. As a result of its flexibility and diversity, African spirituality has spread to different regions around the world, like Europe and the United States. There are communities in various countries that practice African spirituality, like Yoruba, along with other spiritual beliefs from different cultures. This allows for diversity in African spiritual customs and beliefs.

All types of African spirituality share some common beliefs. One of these beliefs is the concept of the afterlife. They believe that death isn't the end of one's journey as there is life after death but in a different realm. This is where their ancestors exist and where the spirits of the dead can live on. This makes death desirable as they spend eternity with the ancestors they revere. Another belief in African spirituality related to death is the concept of reincarnation.

Reincarnation is the rebirth of the soul. Since the soul is eternal and doesn't die, unlike the body, it can begin another journey through rebirth. In other words, the soul is reborn as another human, an animal, a spirit, or a vegetable. That said, the details of how a soul comes back to life vary from belief to belief. For instance, the Yoruba people, specifically in West Africa, believe that a person can be incarnated if they had unfinished business before they died or weren't buried properly. Accordingly, the newly reincarnated person is frequently named after the deceased person.

Since Africans believe in the afterlife and regard death as a happy occasion, their burial rites and preparation of the deceased for the afterlife are significant. Although not all ethnic groups share the same burial traditions, they still all hold this occasion in very high regard. For instance, a group in Kenya called the Abaluya buries their dead naked. Since they regard transitioning to the afterlife as a form of rebirth, they prepare their dead for this moment by burying them naked like a baby. An appropriate burial is vital for the spirit's transition to the afterlife. If a deceased person doesn't get an appropriate burial, their spirits are doomed to wander the physical world and aren't allowed to transition to the next realm. These spirits will never be at peace, and they punish everyone for it by wreaking havoc, causing serious diseases, and becoming evil.

Sometimes, an inappropriate burial rite can be done on purpose as a punishment to the deceased. If the deceased wasn't a good person or didn't lead an honest or kind existence, they are usually given an incomplete burial. All followers of African spirituality desire nothing more than to cross this realm to go to the next and become highly revered ancestors. Therefore, an incomplete burial is a perfect punishment for bad people. Arriving in the afterlife doesn't necessarily mean the deceased is safe from judgment. They are often judged for everything they did when they were alive to determine if they should be rewarded or punished. This belief is meant to encourage people to be good to one another. The people of Yoruba were among those who believed the deceased were either punished or rewarded in the afterlife. However, there are groups in Kenya who believe that an afterlife is a place in another realm where you continue living your life; your spirit continues living in another realm. There is no punishment or reward.

Now that you have familiarized yourself with the basics of African spirituality, we will focus on the different African practices in the next part of the chapter.

Yoruba

The Yoruba religion is one of the oldest beliefs in the world; it even predates Christianity by centuries. It is based on songs, legends, myths, and proverbs taken from West African culture. Yoruba culture originated in West Nigeria about 5,000 years ago, and most of its followers still live in Nigeria. However, there are a few groups that live in Togo and Benin. The people of Yoruba worship the supreme deity and the creator Olodumare, and they refer to themselves, the worshippers, as children. They are also strong believers in the Orishas and the concept of reincarnation. In the last few years, West African culture has seen a resurgence in countries like the United States, the Caribbean, and Canada. In fact, it's estimated that about 500,000 people in different cities around the United States practice the Yoruba religion.

The Yoruba people are one of the largest ethnic groups in Africa. There isn't just one ethnic group in Yoruba culture, but multiple groups. They are diverse people who share the same culture, history, and language. According to Yoruba mythology, the people of Yoruba all descend from their divine king Oduduwa. Like every culture and religion, the Yoruba have their own creation myth and believe that Olorun was the creator of the universe.

After various religions came to Africa, the practice of the Yoruba religion decreased significantly. Yet, about 20% of the people of Yoruba still practice their ancestors' religion. Not all groups follow the same practices, though. For instance, some groups worship a male deity, while others worship a female deity.

There are a few main gods in Yoruba spiritual practice. The first is Olodumare, who is the creator and the sky god. His worshippers call on him by offering prayers which the Orisha usually receive. They can also call on him by pouring water on kola nuts. Olodumare's divine messenger is called Legba or Eshu. Eshu's job is to deliver the sacrifice left by worshippers at Olodumare's shrine. All worshippers pray to Eshu. Another deity is Ifa, who is the god of divination. He interprets Olodumare's wishes and delivers them to the believers.

When the worshippers find themselves struggling and needing help, they often pray to Ifa.

Ogun, the god of war, metalwork, and hunting, is one of the most important gods in the Yoruba religion. According to Yoruba practices, when someone is supposed to give a testimonial, they have to swear to tell the truth by kissing a machete that is sacred to Ogun. The last significant deity in Yoruba's spiritual belief system is Shango, the god of thunder. Shango, the god of thunder, is the final major deity in Yoruba spiritual belief. The people of Yoruba believe that lightning and thunder occur when Shango throws a thunderstone to earth. According to their beliefs, this isn't an ordinary thunderstone; it has special powers. This is why religious leaders roam the streets after thunderstorms looking for this magic thunderstone.

There are several festivals in the Yoruba religion. Honoring the supreme god and the Orishas is one of their main events. Other celebrations include offering sacrifices to their deities so the gods bless them with a good harvest and plentiful rain. During the obligatory festivals, participants reenact different myths and folktales from Yoruba mythology and have a great deal of fun. It is considered a sign of disrespect to the gods, spirits, and ancestors if followers don't attend the festivals and celebrate them.

The Yoruba people are firm believers in reincarnation, and they regard it as a positive experience and even a privilege that is only bestowed on good and kind people who lead honest lives.

Santeria

Santeria originated in West Africa among the people of Yoruba. However, it is considered an Afro-Cuban religion. Through the years, it spread to different countries around the world, like Cuba, Haiti, Puerto Rico, Brazil, Trinidad, and the United States. Santeria is often referred to as Regla de Ocha or the Lucumí, which are the names that their practitioners prefer. The word Santeria is Spanish and loosely translates to "devotion to the saints." This name is appropriate as the practitioners of Santeria refer to their gods and Orishas as saints.

This spiritual practice consists of more than one religious belief. In fact, it is a blend of various cultures and faiths. Interestingly, many of them are extremely different and even contradict each other. As mentioned, African spirituality is diverse, and Santeria is the biggest proof of this diversity. This practice has borrowed elements from different cultures and spiritual faiths worldwide, like Yoruba, Catholicism, and Caribbean traditions. It is also influenced by several African cultures like Senegal, Bantu, and Guinea Coast.

This belief is different and fairly complex because it blends two different faiths with each other, the Orishas of Yoruba and Catholic saints. Santeria has even associated each of their Orishas with a Catholic saint. It's not only a spiritual practice; magic also plays a major role in this belief. Practitioners of Santeria also practice magic. However, their magic is closely related to their understanding and interactions with the Orishas.

Voodoo

What is the first thing that comes to mind when you see the word "voodoo"? Most people, even those unfamiliar with African spirituality, have heard the word voodoo more than once in their lives. If you heard about voodoo from a movie or a TV show, then you probably associate it with black magic, zombies, or devil worship. However, this is an unfair stereotype which is why voodoo is considered the most misunderstood religion. Unfortunately, voodoo has a very sinister reputation. It has been linked to witchcraft and evil spells in the last couple of centuries. With the popularity of some aspects of this practice, like the voodoo doll, most people's idea of what voodoo is has been manipulated by the media. This has put its practitioners in a very precarious position, constantly defending their beliefs and dealing with other people's distrust.

There is no need to be afraid of voodoo. It's time to unlearn everything you know about this practice and approach it with a fresh perspective. You should first be aware that voodoo has nothing to do with demonic worship and isn't a branch of witchcraft. It is a spiritual belief that is no different from Yoruba and Santeria and is not associated with anything evil. The religion originated in Haiti and later spread to different African regions and blended with Catholicism.

Voodoo, which is also spelled *vodou* or *vodun*, is one of the oldest religions in the world, with origins dating back 6,000 years. When voodoo became a part of the modern world, it borrowed elements from Catholicism and African magical and religious rites. It isn't easy to define voodoo or to put it in a category because of its dynamic nature. You may even find two temples in the same village, each with its traditions. That said, there are still some similarities between voodoo traditions. Many of its African elements are borrowed from Yoruba, the Kongo people, the Ewe people, and Fon. Similar to other beliefs, voodoo has changed over the years, yet it still maintains many elements of African spirituality. The people still worship their ancestors and perform transcendental dancing and drumming. Voodoo is practiced in different countries around the world: The Caribbean, Haiti, and New Orleans.

If you watch any movie that features voodoo, you will notice that it is portrayed as something closely related to dark magic with the purpose of harming others. This is clearly a misconception, but what has brought it on? Well, this isn't merely a Hollywood creation. There was a specific incident that took place in 1791 in Haiti. A group of people came upon a voodoo ceremony and believed that what they witnessed was people making deals with the devil. This story is still alive today, with many people acknowledging it. In fact, some people believe the 2010 earthquake that struck Haiti resulted from this deal with the devil that cursed the people of Haiti.

The voodoo followers believe in one supreme deity, which they call Bondye. The deity shares similarities with the Catholic god. They also had their own version of the Orishas, which were gods who were not as powerful as the god they called Iwa. The people who believed in the Iwa made an offering of food and other pleasing objects. These offerings are made when followers need Iwa's assistance. When they want to talk to an Iwa, they hold ceremonies and ask it to take over one of the people there. The followers also use voodoo dolls to attract an Iwa. However, the concept of poking voodoo dolls isn't associated with the voodoo spiritual practice.

Hoodoo

Since voodoo and hoodoo have similar spelling, you may think that they share some similarities. However, the two practices don't have many things in common. Voodoo has its own religious leaders, and its followers usually perform specific practices. The followers also highly revere certain deities and spirits. On the other hand, hoodoo couldn't be more different from anything that voodoo represents. Unlike voodoo and the other practices mentioned here, hoodoo followers don't worship any specific deities. They can worship any god they choose or even choose not to worship any. There is also no hierarchy associated with this religion, and its worshippers don't have to follow a specific structure.

Hoodoo isn't a religion that everyone can practice since only Black people are allowed to practice it. It began as a way to help Black people overcome the trauma they had experienced as enslaved people. To this day, Black people practice hoodoo to protect themselves from all the dangers they encounter daily.

African spirituality has a rich and fascinating history. This belief is very tolerant of other religions that it meets along the way. It borrowed elements from many religions, which allowed for a diverse belief system to evolve that many people gravitate toward. There is still much more to discuss about African spirituality. This chapter has only scratched the surface. In the next chapter, you'll learn about the supreme deity Oldumare and the creation myth.

Chapter 2: Olodumare, the Supreme God

With few exceptions, every culture in the world has come up with its own myth about creation. It's a fundamental and universal question: how did the world come to be? Because people don't believe that the world just appeared out of nowhere, someone must have created it. When they couldn't find an explanation, many cultures decided to come up with their own interpretation. African culture is no different; it has created its own myth to help explain how the universe and mankind came into existence.

Priests in their temple.
Creator: Dierk Lange, CC0, via Wikimedia Commons:
https://commons.wikimedia.org/wiki/File:Obatala_Priester_im_Tempel.jpg

Most creation myths have the same elements. They are usually supernatural stories that revolve around the culture's mythology and include multiple religious' themes. These stories explain how the earth, humanity, and the universe were created. Usually, one or more deities are involved in creating the universe. The most dominating themes in these stories are usually one of the following: creating the universe out of nothing, two parents' deities separating, or a land appearing from an infinite ocean.

You can learn so much about a culture from its creation story. Although the events in these stories aren't necessarily real or factual, they still reflect the culture's beliefs. However, some of these beliefs are expressed on a symbolic level. The African creation myth will help you better understand your culture's history and learn about the supreme being, Olodumare, and his role in creating the universe.

The Myth of Creation

In the beginning, before mankind came to be, the universe looked nothing like it does today. There was only darkness, except for a translucent layer that stood out in the darkness. It was a small land that laid the foundations for the universe's birth. Inside the translucent layer were space, air, water, and light. This layer was the home of Olodumare. He created light and ordered it to spread over the universe. Although there was light, the world was still empty, leaving room for plenty more creations, something that Obatala was beginning to realize.

There was only the sky up above, wild marshlands below, and water. Olodumare was the supreme god who ruled the sky, and his twin sister Olokun was an Orisha spirit and the sea goddess. Although both siblings were twins, they were, in fact, estranged. One day, the god Obatala, who was also one of the greatest Orishas, reflected on the state of his existence and the world around him. He was bored and restless with his existence in his heavenly home. Obatala believed that this world could be more than it was. He decided to create another world but wanted to get Olodumare's permission first. Obatala went to Olodumare and told him that he wanted to create a dry land with fields, mountains, forests, and valleys so all living creatures could live on it. Olodumare liked Obatala's idea and granted him instant permission.

Obatala was very excited to start creating his new world. However, he didn't know where to start, and he had a few questions that he wanted answers to before he headed off on his new adventure. Obtala wasn't stubborn; in fact, he was rather intelligent. He was aware that he wasn't all-knowing and saw no shame in consulting someone who had more knowledge than him. Obatala sought the advice of Orunmila, the god of prophecy and Olodumare's oldest son. Orunmila told him that he would need a long golden chain to help him reach the world below. Obatala went to a goldsmith to make him the chain. The goldsmith agreed but said that Obatala must provide the gold. He went to all the gods, asking them for gold, and they were all happy to help him. He delivered the gold, and the goldsmith created the chain for him. Orunmila also told Obatala that he would need a black cat, a white hen, a palm nut, and a snail shell that he must fill with sand from the heavens, put them in a bag, and carry them on his journey down below. Orunmila helped Obatala to obtain all these items. With the help of the gods and Orunmila, Obatala was ready for his journey.

Orunmila advised Obatala to take another Orisha to help him, so he chose Oduduwa. Now they were both ready for the trip. Obatala used the golden chain to climb down from the heavens. However, he realized that the chain wasn't long enough, and he still had a short distance to go. Orunmila helped Obatala from heaven and told him to begin using the items in his bag. He was first instructed to throw the sand in the snail's shell on Earth and then release the hen. The hen scattered the sand, and it began forming the land. Obatala and Oduduwa finally descended on the earth and called the place where they landed Ife. The land kept expanding thanks to heaven's sand and the hen.

Obatala and Oduduwa spent some time in Ife with the black cat to keep them company. Obatala planted the palm nut, which immediately grew into a palm tree. Palm nuts dropped from this tree on the ground, and they all grew immediately. Now Obatala had his own forest of palm trees all around him. He then wanted a place to settle, so he built himself a hut. Obatala lived in the hut with the black cat. He had a daily routine, and he was enjoying his new life. But after a few months, Obatala became lonely and bored. He decided that he wanted to be around other beings like him so he could interact with them, and they would keep him company. Obatala was a talented sculptor, so he used his skill to make clay figures of beings like him. He began sculpting, but after some time, he grew tired, so he took a break and drank some wine. He got drunk, but he continued creating his clay figures. After he was done, he asked Olodumare to breathe life into them so they could come alive.

The next day, Obatala was shocked to find that the beings he created when he was drunk were all deformed. Obtala was ashamed of what he had done and vowed never to have a sip of wine again. He decided that he would become the protector of the deformed to make up for his mistake.

After seeing what Obatala had created, Oduduwa decided to create his own beings, but he wanted them to be better formed than those that Obatala had created. He sought Olodumare's help. Oduduwa created mankind with the help of the supreme god. Oduduwa loved human beings, so he decided to live among them and become their king instead of going back to heaven. His children and grandchildren populated Yoruba and created more kingdoms.

Olodumare

Olodumare was the lord of the heavens, and he ruled over 17,000 divinities that existed in the pantheon of Yoruba. It is clear from the myth of creation that neither the world nor human beings would have existed if it weren't for Olodumare. He gave his permission to Obatala to create the world and helped him and Oduduwa to create mankind by breathing life into them. Although Obatala and Oduduwa did most of the work, none of it would have happened without the supreme god lending a hand. Olodumare was the supreme god/being of Yoruba. According to the people of Yoruba, he was one of the first beings to exist, and he created heaven and earth, day and night, and the four seasons. The fate of mankind is in Olodumare's hands, but he is a fair deity. When someone makes a mistake, the Orishas usually handle their punishment. Olodumare judges people differently, though. He doesn't only look at their actions, but he also considers their personality, character, and inner feelings. Olodumare knows each person's true self, so he looks into their hearts before he judges their actions.

When a person dies, their soul must stand before Olodumare and be judged. He judges mankind based on their morals. If the person has been good in their life, they receive rewards from Olodumare. Olodumare rules over heaven and earth, so he judges all beings in both worlds, including the Orishas. His will must always be done, and no creature in heaven or on earth can go against it. He is the one in control of everything in the universe, which is why all beings abide by his will.

Olodumare and the Orisha aren't the same, and one main thing sets them apart. Olodumare is a supreme being, not just a regular deity, unlike the Orisha. He represents the natural force of life, a higher form of humanity, and a pure concept of human nature. Although both Olodumare and the Orishas play major roles in the Yoruba religion, Olodumare has a more significant role. He is a more complex being, and no mortal is able or allowed to see Olodumare.

Unlike other deities, there aren't temples in which to worship Olodumare. There also aren't any priests devoted to this supreme deity. According to the Yoruba religion, all priests highly revere Olodumare and give him offerings. There is a group of priests called the Oracle of Ifa, who have the required skills to understand and interpret Olodumare's words. Olodumare also communicates his will to the devoted followers of Orisha Orunmila, who is also the god of wisdom.

Death wasn't a concept in the Yoruba religion, as it didn't exist at first. People didn't die, but they kept growing until they became huge. They then began shrinking until they became weak and old. According to legend, mankind grew tired of living such long lives, and since death didn't exist, the region became overpopulated. They prayed to Olodumare to liberate them from these long lives, and he answered their prayers by creating death. Just like Olodumare breathed life into mankind, he created what can take life away - death. He is the creator of everything and is revered for his knowledge and wisdom. Since he is the supreme god, no deity is wiser or more powerful than him. He isn't a passive god who just watches mankind from the heavens. Olodumare plays a significant role in the destinies of all beings in heaven and on earth, yet he never directly interferes. Olodumare often depends on the Orishas to handle mankind's prayers or concerns.

Olodumare resembles the concept of god found in Judaism, Christianity, and Islam. This deity has been around since the beginning of time – possibly even before, since he has no beginning and no end. He is and will always be present. Although he lives in the sky, Olodumare is everywhere and the source of life. All that was, all that is, and all that will be, comes from him. The simple human brain can't comprehend or conceptualize the concept of Olodumare.

At night, when the world goes to sleep, Olodumare is the one who is in charge and handles all the hopes and dreams of his creation. Olodumare wasn't born since he didn't have any parents. Most gods in other cultures are often illustrated so that people can understand and have an idea of what they look like. However, there aren't any images of this deity, just like there aren't any shrines or devoted priests. This means that Olodumare isn't worshiped directly - even sacrifices aren't made directly to him. The Orishas often act as the "middle man," receiving the people's prayers or sacrifice instead of Olodumare. In fact, Olodumare prefers to keep a distance from mankind. However, there are some of his followers who directly worship him. When a person is in trouble, they call on the Orishas for assistance. However, sometimes the Orishas refuse to help or may lack the ability or power to assist in a particular issue. In this case, the people will have no other choice but to call on Olodumare directly.

Olodumare didn't always keep his distance from mankind. In fact, once upon a time, the earth was in very close proximity to Olodumare and the sky. However, mankind offended Olodumare by eating from the sky. He decided to keep his distance from them and the earth. This is why the sky is now far away from earth.

As the creator of everything, he is also considered the source of mortality and virtue. When a child is born, Olodumare bestows upon them his knowledge. He is the most powerful being with superior knowledge, yet he has the capacity for good and evil.

Olodumare is a just and fair god, but he doesn't suffer disrespect or bad behavior lightly. According to a Yoruba myth, at one time, Olodumare wasn't happy with how the Orishas were behaving. He didn't want to destroy them and decided that punishment and teaching them a lesson was the better option. He prevented the sky from raining and let the Orishas suffer a drought so they could learn from their mistakes. The Orishas were struggling and sought Olodumare's forgiveness. They tried to call on him and reach out to him, but he was too high in the sky and couldn't or wouldn't hear them. One of the Orishas, Oshun, transformed into a peacock and volunteered to fly to heaven and beg Olodumare to return the rain. However, on her way up, she lost her feathers and became a vulture. She kept flying until she reached him. Olodumare appreciated the sacrifice and what she had endured on her trip to meet him. He brought back the rain, and as a reward for her sacrifice, he made Oshun his messenger. To this day, there are still people in Yoruba who worship Olodumare.

Olodumare, Olorun, and Olofi

Olodumare means the almighty and supreme, Olorun means the owner, and Olofin-Orun means the lord of heaven. According to the Yoruba religion, Olodumare was the creator and supreme god. Olofin came before him, and he ruled over everything that existed in the universe. Olofin was also responsible for the Orishas and had power over them. The Orishas aren't allowed to take action with matters concerning the earth without going to Olofin first. Olodumare, Olorun, and Olofi are all manifestations of the deity. They represent three stages, the universe, the creation of man, and everything that takes place on earth.

Olofin and Olrun are Olodumare's other names. In Yoruba mythology, these three names represent different aspects of the same deity. The concept is similar to that of the Holy Trinity in Catholicism. In fact, the followers of the Santeria wanted to come up with a concept similar to the Holy Trinity. It's basically three individuals/beings who have the same essence.

Olodumare

This is the spiritual manifestation of the deity. In this stage, he is the creator who breathes life into all living things.

Olorun

This manifestation of the deity spreads supreme energy that facilitates the continuation of life on earth. Olorun is often represented by the sun, which also emits energy responsible for all life on earth.

Olofin

The people of Yoruba use this term to refer to their king, the manifestation closest to the Orishas and mankind. It represents the manifestation of the god on earth. According to the Yoruba religion, Olofin is their patriarch. When he wants to come down to earth, he often transforms into energy. He is the keeper of all secrets related to creation.

Olodumare in African Spirituality

Olodumare and his manifestations play a huge role in the practices of African Spirituality, Yoruba, Santeria, Voodoo, and Hoodoo. Voodoo is a monotheistic religion which means that its followers worship one god. This god is Olorun in Yoruba culture. Olodumare is highly revered and regarded as a supreme deity in all faiths. In the Yoruba religion, followers don't offer sacrifices to Olodumare, but they offer them to the Orishas. In Yoruba and Santeria, there aren't any symbols or statues of Olodumare. However, he was still highly revered. In Santeria, Olodumare is in first place on their religious hierarchy.

It is obvious from everything mentioned so far that Olodumare was a good deity. He supported both Obatala and Oduduwa to create the world and mankind. Instead of destroying the Orishas, he opted for punishment to help them learn their lesson. He is fair and just and looks at the person's character and heart before he punishes mankind. It makes sense for Olodumare to be highly revered among different religions in African spirituality.

Olodumare created the universe and breathed his life into mankind, making him the most significant being in all African religions. Now that you have learned about the supreme being Olodumare, you'll enter the world of the Orishas in the next chapters. They have a prominent role in African spirituality and aided Olodumare in creating the universe.

Chapter 3: Who Are the Orishas?

The Yoruba people of West Africa are among the most populous and widespread African ethnicities. Their culture is rich in art, music, and traditions. The Yoruba people also have a unique spiritual system known as Orisha worship. Orisha worship, sometimes called Orisa, centers on spirits known as Orishas. These Orishas are manifestations of nature and forces that help keep the balance of life on Earth. Moreover, they are the only conduit through which God's energy flows and the only way humans can communicate directly with him. Each Orisha has different responsibilities, characteristics, and personality traits. This chapter will delve into Orisha's origin and its significance in African spirituality.

Orishas are manifestations of nature and forces that help keep the balance of life on Earth.
Omoeko Media, CC BY-SA 4.0 <https://creativecommons.org/licenses/by-sa/4.0>, via Wikimedia Commons: https://commons.wikimedia.org/wiki/File:Orishas_in_Oba%27s_palace,_Abeokuta.jpg

Who Are the Orishas?

In the African diaspora, Orishas are a group of deities that have found significant representation among the descendants of enslaved Africans. African culture is filled with stories of spirits, gods, and goddesses. These are the powerful forces that make up the Orishas. Orishas are found to exist in many different cultures throughout Africa. They represent natural forces and can be found everywhere, from rivers to trees to rocks. Although most people do not commonly know them outside of Africa, you can meet them wherever you go. These beings are described in various ways, which is indicative of their omnipotence.

Orishas are divine beings believed to guide the world and provide guidance to followers. The Yoruba people believe in a pantheon of different Orishas responsible for different realms in life. Some Orishas are responsible for health and healing, while others oversee love, money, and social justice. Orishas are believed to have both positive and negative characteristics, and followers can tap into the Orishas' powers to help with different areas in their lives. Orishas are also referred to as gods and goddesses, the chief difference being that the Orishas are seen as nature deities who govern and control the forces of nature. The Orishas are seen as ancestors who were kings and queens of the ancient Yoruba civilization. Orishas are worshiped as supreme deities of the Yoruba people. Their shrines are found in houses, vernacular shrines, and churches. Orishas are associated with specific aspects of life, such as love, war, fertility, music, and many other parts.

The Orishas are also known as spirits who have survived in various forms throughout Africa. They have been worshiped as gods and goddesses. Still, they have also been recognized as natural forces and energies that regulate life on the planet. This is a very old practice and can be traced back to the beginning of human culture. It is easy to dismiss spiritual practices as outdated and irrelevant, but they are still alive today. If you are looking for a unique spiritual practice, Orisha worship may be a good fit for you.

What Religions Believe in the Orishas?

Although Orisha worship is most commonly associated with the Yoruba people, many African and Latin American religions believe in the Orishas. In fact, they were originally the objects of a Hindu spiritual practice before being adopted into the Yoruba people's beliefs. Orisha worship is most popular in Brazil, Cuba, Puerto Rico, and Haiti. However, you may also find practitioners in other parts of Latin America and in western African countries like Nigeria and Ghana. Orisha worship is also commonly associated with Santeria, a combination of Yoruba beliefs with Catholic and Animist practices.

You might have heard of the Lwa. Also called Loa or Loi. Lwa spirits are part of the African diasporic religion of Haitian Vodou. Much like the Orishas, Lwa are deities whose identities are derived from traditional African religions. As opposed to Yoruba gods (Orisha), the Loa are spirits of voodoo. The Orishas are gods in their own right and answer only to the divine being and creator, Olodumare.

The Importance of Orisha in African Spirituality

The Yoruba people have had a profound impact on the world. Not only did they create beautiful art and music, but they also developed spirituality and rituals that would influence other cultures and religions. Orisha worship is the most prominent spiritual practice that came from the Yoruba people. The worship of Orisha spirits from the Yoruba religion is called Orisha-Ifa. Orisha-Ifa is an ancient spiritual practice that the Yoruba people have practiced for hundreds of years. Orisha-Ifa is based on the philosophy that everything in the universe is interrelated. The Orishas are spirits and energies that keep the balance of life on Earth. Orisha-Ifa is a way to communicate and tap into the Orisha spirits to help with life.

The Orishas are responsible for helping humanity and providing guidance to the people that worship them. However, the Orishas only help people who try to communicate with them. People who worship the Orishas are expected to make sacrifices to them to show respect. Followers must also maintain a strong, honest code of moral conduct and follow strict guidelines to receive help from the Orishas.

The Orishas and Spirituality

Spirituality is a word that is often associated with religion. But spirituality and religion are not the same things. Religion is often defined as a belief system connecting people to a higher power (as in a god). Spirituality, on the other hand, is a journey to find meaning and purpose in life. It's about finding one's own connection to a higher power. Orisha worship is the spiritual practice of the Yoruba people, but it's not a religion. The Yoruba people do not believe in one true god but in many gods that can be found worldwide. Orisha worship is a way to tap into a higher power and get guidance and advice on how to best navigate life.

In Practice

Because the Orishas are deities that represent natural forces and principles, through their stories and teachings that illustrate how humans should live to please them, they serve to reinforce social norms. Orishas also play an important role in healing. People who practice Ifa usually visit Ifa priests to consult them about their problems. During the consultation, the Ifa priest will advise on how to solve the problem or how to cope with the situation if that is not possible. Orishas also provide inspiration when a person is feeling depressed or in need of motivation. Orishas inspire people to live a life connected to nature and the universe, and they will be healthy and live a fulfilling life.

Orisha Beliefs

The Orishas can be both benevolent and malicious. They rule over different parts of life, and their moods can change depending on the day. Orisha worshipers must take these mood swings into account when communicating with them. Orisha worshipers also believe that a parallel realm of spirits exists alongside humans. There is a set of rules and limitations in this realm, and humans can tap into these spirits to help with life. Depending on where an Orisha is coming from, they can either help or hurt humans. An Orisha coming from a negative place can harm humans if left unchecked. But an Orisha coming from a positive place can help humanity immensely.

In Practice

Orishas represent natural forces and principles, such as fate, fertility, love, war, or healing. They also serve to reinforce social norms through their stories and teachings that illustrate how humans should live to please them. Orishas are similar to the gods of other religions in that they are immortal, superhuman entities that can be either beneficent or malevolent toward humankind. However, the Orisha consciousness does not exist independently of human consciousness. Every Orisha has a human counterpart, called an Orisha-head, through whom they can live and contact the physical world. This human counterpart can be a living person or someone who has died. Orishas are often associated with colors, foods, and numbers. They have distinct personalities and temperaments and can be either hot-tempered or cool-headed. They can also be either white or black, good or evil.

How to Worship the Orishas

The best way to worship the Orishas is to tap into the powers of each Orisha. To do this, you first invite an Orisha into your body by drinking a libation (usually a type of alcohol). When you drink an Orisha libation, you can expect them to come into your body within 30 minutes. After you invite an Orisha into your body, create a ritual to invite them into your life. You can do this by burning incense or by lighting candles. You can also write down what you want to accomplish in life or which Orisha you want to invite into your body.

Exploring the Classification of Orisha

The classification of Orishas was serious for the Yoruba people because it helped them logically organize the deities. It also gave the people an idea about how to interact with them through the Ifa system. The Ifa system is a complex system that uses various symbols and colors to understand the world and communicate with the Orishas.

How Many Orisha Are There?

There are hundreds of Orishas, and their number is continuously growing. However, when the Orishas were first brought to Africa, they were part of a small group of deities. With the evolution of the Ifa tradition, the number of Orishas grew. As the Orishas were worshiped, they were given new names and were associated with different aspects of the natural world and human life. Orishas were also combined with each other or with others to create new deities. More deities were added to the pantheon as time passed because people needed new Orishas to worship. New deities were also created to represent natural phenomena that were not previously part of the Ifa tradition.

The number of Orishas varies between and within the sources. According to the Orisha religion, there are 400 - 1,440 Orishas. Different communities and scholars have given different numbers, but they all agree it is very high. According to the Encyclopedia Britannica, there are more than 600 Orishas. The encyclopedia claims that it is impossible to know the exact number of Orishas because the Orisha religion is an oral tradition passed down from generation to generation.

What Are the Different Types of Orishas?

The different types of Orishas are complex questions, and there isn't a single answer. The question often depends on whom you ask and what source you are looking at. According to the Orisha religion, the classification and the number of Orishas are not fixed. The types of Orishas change over time, and the people who interact with them also change. So, it is impossible to say that there is a single correct classification of Orishas. However, there are many Orishas who are commonly known and worshiped. Some of the most important gods and goddesses are Oshun, Ogun, Yemaya, and Eshu. Oshun is the goddess of love and beauty, Ogun is the god of iron, the forge, and weapons, Yemoja is the goddess of the sea, and Eshu is the god of communication, luck, and chaos.

The dark or hot-tempered Orisha is a god or goddess who is connected to the concepts of disorder, chaos, and destruction. These Orishas are associated with the sun and the color red or black. The dark Orishas are often feared and misunderstood by those who don't understand the Orisha religion. They are often considered evil, but actually, they are concerned with destroying evil.

- **Eshu:** Male deity (red and black)
- **Ogun:** Male deity (dark green or blue, and black)
- **Shango:** Male deity (red and white)
- **Oya:** Female deity (red)

They symbolize fire, volcanoes, and the masculine principle. As well as representing the destructive powers of the Earth, they can also be both kind and frightening. Volcanoes and earthquakes are closely linked to these deities. Transformation, death, and rebirth are also important powers of the darker Orishas.

The white or cool-tempered Orisha is a spirit connected to the concept of justice, peace, and order. They are concerned with the imposition of order, which is why they are often connected to the kings and queens who rule over these kingdoms. White Orishas are associated with water, the moon, and lighter colors like white. They are usually kind and loving. They are usually the Orishas of priests because the priests are concerned with the order of the spiritual world.

- **Orunmila:** Male deity (white)
- **Obatala:** Male deity (white)
- **Erinle:** Male deity (green, yellow, coral)
- **Yemoja:** Female deity (white and blue)

They are the creators of the Earth, and all of nature, with Eshu being the creator of the human species. White Orishas focus on the positive things in life. They dislike negativity and sustain their power through love, joy, and peace. These deities are also closely connected to the Earth's natural forces, like water, wind, and the feminine principle.

Understanding the Terminology of African Spirituality and Orishas

When it comes to African spirituality and orishas, there's a lot that can be confusing for those who are new to the topic. You likely need a bit more help understanding a few of the core concepts. We understand that this can be a little bit frustrating, especially if you're interested in learning more about them. After all, who wouldn't want to learn more about something that intrigues you so much?

How Does One Work with the Orishas?

Orishas are the spirits of nature and human life. They are both the giver and the taker of life. They are the guardians of our world and our lives and are always ready to help us. The best way to work with the Orishas is by communicating with them and making offerings of gratitude or requests for their assistance. Orishas love to be acknowledged and thanked for their presence and assistance. They also love to be acknowledged for the gifts that they have given us. If you want to work with the Orishas, it is best to meditate regularly to open a channel of communication and to start to learn about their names, symbols, and characteristics. Regularly reading about the Orishas is also very helpful in furthering your connection to them.

Ashe

When presented with the entity of Ashe, Orishas can carry out their missions using the positive energy that is present in the world. As a result of their energy and power, Orishas can give blessings, create miracles, and dispel misfortune in the world. Ashe can be compared to the concept of divine power and energy found in many religions. Orishas use this power to create miracles, promote changes, and dispel evil.

Ebbo

Ebbo is an offering and sacrifice to the Orishas. It is a gift to show them respect, gratitude, and love. Ebbo can be any gift that you feel comfortable giving to the Orishas. This can include items like food, beverages, incense, animals, flowers, and more. Ebbo is practiced regularly by those who work with the Orishas. It is a way to show your respect, love, and gratitude to the Orishas and other spiritual beings helping you.

Can Orisha Get Offended?

Yes. But we can't generalize and say that all Orishas get offended. We have to look at the specific Orisha for the answer. Each Orisha has its own special personality, likes, and dislikes. They are also living entities that are capable of feeling emotions just like we are. Just like we get offended, so do the Orishas.

How Can I Make Sure Not to Offend an Orisha?

If you don't want to offend an Orisha, there are a few ways to avoid doing so. First, you want to determine which Orisha you are interested in working with. Once you have decided which one you want to work with, you want to learn as much as possible about them. Then when you've done the background homework, you can start to ensure that you don't offend them. One thing that you can do is to make sure to always be respectful of Orisha. Show them the love and gratitude you want others to show you. Suppose you have a specific Orisha that you want to work with. In that case, it is important to understand that they have their own personalities, likes, and dislikes.

When Am I Ready to Connect with a Certain Orisha?

As with most things involving spirituality, there is no "one size fits all" method when connecting with an Orisha. However, some general guidelines can help you along the way. Look for signs indicating when you are ready to connect with a particular Orisha. Some of them include your purpose in life, how comfortable you feel with yourself and others, what you want to achieve, your level of confidence as well as your beliefs. For example, if you are unsure of who you are or what you want out of life, then it would be best to wait until you can figure those things out first. On the other hand, if you are clear on what you want and where you want to be in life, then it could be a good time to start connecting with Orisha. It all depends on where you are on your journey.

What Signs Do Orishas Give?

To see signs from an Orisha, look for any corresponding behavior that matches the description given in prayers. For example, suppose you are praying to Yemoja. In that case, you may notice that you have a strong maternal instinct or that your body feels lighter during menstruation as a sign of your devotion to this goddess.

The most common signs of an Orisha include:

- A strong sense of community or belonging
- An increased interest in spirituality or religion
- A feeling of being protected or safe
- A sudden and overwhelming need to do good deeds or help people in need

Do I Need to Be Initiated into an African Religion before Attempting Communication with the Orishas?

There is no requirement for initiation into an African religion. If you are sincerely interested in contacting the Orishas, it is best to do so while mentally and emotionally calm. The only requirement is that you have an open heart, willingness, and desire to learn about and respect the Orishas. Most people who work with the Orishas do so on their own after feeling the call of the spirit in some way. Others are initiated into a religion by a trusted friend or family member who shares a close bond with the Orisha they want to commune with.

Many become familiar with traditional African religions to cultivate spiritual awareness, practice gratitude, and deepen their connection with nature. In addition, some people find it helpful to use traditional practices as a form of prayer – seeking guidance from the divine but still remaining in control of their practice by making daily choices aligned with their personal beliefs and values.

Chapter 4: The White Orishas

There are many Orishas — some say there are hundreds of them. However, most of them can be grouped into four main families. The Red Orishas (warrior spirits), the White Orishas (peaceful spirits), the Blue-Green Orishas (nature spirits), and the Black Orishas (royal spirits). In the Yoruba religion, each deity has a distinct role and responsibility regarding natural elements like water, earth, fire, and air. This chapter will examine the most prominent white Orishas, exploring their main characteristics. Some suggested deities in this category are Orunmila, Obatala, Yemaya, Osain, Oshumare, Oshosi, Oshun, and Olokun. Collectively, they are known as the white Orishas because their colors contrast the colors of other Orishas. And most especially because their characteristics represent purity and peace above all things.

In the Yoruba religion, each deity has a distinct role and responsibility regarding natural elements like water, earth, fire, and air.
Omoeko Media, CC BY-SA 4.0 <https://creativecommons.org/licenses/by-sa/4.0>, via Wikimedia Commons: https://commons.wikimedia.org/wiki/File:Orishas_in_Abeokuta.jpg

Main Characteristics of the White Orishas

Several deities can be classified as white Orishas due to their association with light, purity, and peace. These gods have very different roles from the others within the Yoruba culture. There is an Orisha for everything from love to war, agriculture to hunting and fishing. An Orisha's role is to link heaven and earth, maintain balance in all things, help a person through difficult times, and bring comfort. The white Orishas are considered more benevolent than other Orishas. They can be male or female, though most white Orishas are female. They can take many different forms but are usually depicted as beautiful young women with long flowing hair wearing white dresses, white cloaks, or white beads around their necks. They are often shown to be wearing white robes that shroud their faces in shadows so that they cannot be seen clearly by mortal eyes. They may also wear masks or carry calabashes filled with water or sacred liquids. Their presence can be felt through music, nature, or even in the air itself. White Orishas are also represented in artwork such as paintings, sculptures, and carvings on wood or stone. They appear as guardians of children, heroes, and healers in stories and myths. The white Orishas help people in need by offering guidance, strength, and understanding during difficult times.

Because the white Orishas guard the balance of creation, they inhabit all things and watch over the world at all times. They often appear in visions to those seeking guidance or protection and can be invoked for blessings during rituals and ceremonies. In addition to providing protection against evil, the White Orishas also bless their followers with success.

In order to choose the right Orisha for you to connect with, you'll have to consider all of the different types of Orishas out there. However, if you want to be in touch with Orishas, you should start by getting to know them a little better.

The White Orishas

Each deity has its own individual characteristics. Understanding these groupings helps you better understand the role of each individual Orisha so you can choose the one that best suits you. While some of them may share commonalities, there are subtle differences in how they are perceived. However, just like any other culture or belief system, the main characteristics of these spirits can be narrowed down to a few key points. Next, we'll go over the main characteristics of some of the main white Orishas and explain why they are unique compared to other deities from this religion.

Orunmila (Orúla, Ọrúnla)

Orunmila is the god of knowledge, wisdom, creativity, and justice. He is often illustrated with a staff in his hand, a crown on his head, and a book in his hand. Orunmila is one of the oldest Orisha. Some myths claim that he existed even before the creation of the earth. He is also credited with being the creator of the Santeria Ifa, a set of symbols used when reading the divination system known as Ifa. This deity's name translates to "Owner of the compound" or "Owner of the house."

For modern-day spirituality, Orunmila is a balanced and gentle spirit. He is a great deity to call upon if you need help with a creative project or want to excel in a field that requires knowledge. He can provide you with the guidance and creativity you need to make your dreams a reality. Orunmila is a helpful and patient Orisha who is also extremely generous. He does not have a temper and is rarely angered by other people's actions. He can also help you win any challenge, competition, or situation where you need a bit of luck.

How to Greet Orunmila

Orunmila can be best described as a balanced yet assertive energy. Greet Orunmila with white, yellow, and green, and ensure you are in touch with your emotions and are without judgments in your heart. He is a great source of wisdom and guidance, leading people toward the right choices. Orunmila is the spirit of knowledge, so he is a great deity to call upon if you want to expand your knowledge in a specific field. He can help you grow and understand your strengths and weaknesses. If you need luck, Orunmila can also help you in that area. He can also ease any feelings of anxiety, granting you the ability to cope easily with stressful situations.

Symbols and Ebbo (Sacrificial Ritual)

Orunmila's symbols are a crown, a staff, a book, and a rooster. Orunmila's rooster is a symbol of his connection with the sun. His staff symbolizes Orunmila's abilities with knowledge, abundance, and justice. The staff is an ancient symbol that can be traced back to ancient civilizations. A crown Ebbo is used to call upon his status and the knowledge he holds. A holy book can be used to access the divination system known as Ifa.

Obatala (Oxalá, Ochalá)

Obatala is the god of creation. He is also known for being the Orisha of purity and is often depicted as being very clean and polished. Obatala was one of the first Orisha to emerge. Some myths claim that Orunmila was created from a virgin coconut tree that sprung from a flood. Because he is one of the first, many people consider him a great deity to call upon when starting a new venture or project. It is believed that he can help you create a smooth and successful transition into a new situation.

How to Greet Obatala

The best way to describe Obatala is that he is extremely pure. He keeps everything around him clean and well-organized due to his strong desire for order. Aside from being patient and helpful, Obatala is also a very kind and generous Orisha. He rarely gets offended by other people's actions and doesn't have a temper.

Symbols and Ebbo

Obatala's symbols are a staff, a white crown, and an iridescent white gown. The staff symbolizes Obatala's connection with the sun and the principles of justice. The coconut tree symbolizes Obatala's abilities with creation and new beginnings. It is believed that this tree sprang from the flood, which was the first beginning of the world. Obatala usually receives white animals as offerings, such as pigeons, hens, and goats. He prefers bland food offerings, for example, milk, rice, and white bread. Alcohol should not be included.

Yemaya (Yemoja)

The Orisha Yemaya is the goddess of the ocean. This Orisha symbolizes fertility and growth, representing the ever-changing tides of life. She is considered the mother of the universe and is believed to be the primary force behind creating life. Swans, turtles, and crabs are her sacred animals, and she is associated with the colors white and blue. Yemaya's characteristics include being gentle and compassionate but also having a certain level of toughness when the situation calls for it. She is willing to help anyone who asks for it and expects nothing in return. She is also the guardian of women, babies, and young children. Yemaya performs many rituals relating to the sea, including healing rituals. Additionally, some of her ceremonies are focused on finding lost items.

Her colors (blue and white) symbolize purity, honesty, and simplicity. Yemaya's primary characteristics are her gentle nature and selfless compassion for others. She is also a symbol of fertility and growth, representing the ever-changing tides of life. Her association with the ocean comes from her ability to produce life even in the most extreme circumstances. Yemaya is capable of great things but is also very demanding and expects a lot from people.

How to Greet Yemaya

When greeting Yemaya, remain calm but ready to take action if necessary. Yemaya is not one for small talk, so it would be wise to keep any greeting short. You can start by facing her Ebbo and gently pressing your palms together. After that, you should bow your head to show respect and gratitude. You can say "Ashe" ("be blessed" in Yoruba). After the greeting, you can move on to your request. The ritual can end by thanking her, but without the bow.

Symbols and Ebbo

The symbols that represent Yemaya are the shell, sea sparrow, conch, coconut, ebony, cedarwood, water lily, and swan. All of these items are associated with the sea. The Ebbo that is given to Yemaya consists of anything related to the sea.

Oshun (Osun)

Oshun is the goddess of love, the river, and sweetness. She is the Orisha of the sweet orange in Caribbean and African cuisine. She represents water, a symbol of fertility and abundance. Hence, she is associated with love and marriage and is the protector or nurturer of humanity. Oshun is a motherly figure and also a seductress, as she represents femininity and the unbridled sensuality that comes with it. Her fertility derives from the sweetness of her personality, while her association with love and marriage comes from her connection with the river. Oshun is associated with white, red, and yellow. These colors represent the purity of her heart and her connection with love, fertility, and the river. The Orisha Oshun is strongly associated with the number five and the elements of water, earth, and air.

How to Greet Oshun

Goddess of love, sweetness, and the river. Therefore, when greeting her, it is important to embrace the symbolism of each of these things. When greeting the Orisha, you want to do so with respect and love. Therefore, a great way to greet her is to give a gift. This can be anything from flowers to a nice piece of jewelry.

Symbols and Ebbo

Oshun is strongly associated with the crescent moon, white, the number five, and water, earth, and air elements. Therefore, these items can be used to summon her for blessings and assistance. Using a crescent moon to summon Oshun is as simple as wrapping a white cloth around your body. This will help you tap into her energy and allow her to help you with your problems and issues. Wrap the white cloth around you and use white decorations when summoning her too. And don't forget the number five. Place five things in your summoning area, or have five people present during the ritual. Because water, earth, and air are her elements, as are sunflower, pumpkin, or cinnamon, sprinkle water in the summoning area - specifically outside in the open air.

Osain (Osanyìn)

Osain is the god of the forest, the harvest, and the hunt. He is associated with the color green, red, white, and yellow and the number eight. He is also the Orisha who rules over all of the wild animals. Osain is a fierce warrior who protects his followers and destroys evil spirits. He is a fearsome warrior and a gentle healer. Summon him to heal any ailment, be it physical or mental, and bring you great fortune.

How to Greet Osain

When greeting Osain, it is best to remember that he rules over the forest and is strongly associated with those colors. Therefore, when greeting him, it is a good idea to use forest-specific items and have his colors wrapped around you. This is the best way to greet Osain and get his attention. You don't need to do much because he is known for his rational temperament.

Symbols and Ebbo

Osain is strongly associated with his colors and the number eight. Therefore, these are the perfect symbols to use when summoning him. Clay is a symbol of Osain and can be used to help cleanse your space and remove negative energy before a ritual. Then use eight items for his Ebba, such as plants or twigs.

Oshumare (Oshunmare)

Oshumare is the god of creation and purity. Together with the moon, Oshumare is the patron saint of marriage, sickness, and death. In addition to creating the Earth, Oshumare informs the other Orishas of their responsibilities on the planet. He has the greatest amount of power over the oceans, seas, and all water sources like rivers and lakes. As such, Oshumare is often consulted during the process of divination and when one wishes for knowledge and wisdom. Oshumare is also consulted when one wishes to have a child or trying to conceive.

Oshumare is said to be very wise and kind and has a lot of knowledge to share with those who seek advice from him. He is said to be a passive Orisha, meaning he does not like fighting or having those around him engage in conflict. In fact, Oshumare is a very peaceful Orisha and is the creator of peace and happiness in the world. He is considered a healer and is said to have the power to heal any physical or mental illness that one may experience. He is often illustrated as a smiling Orisha.

How to Greet Oshumare

When greeting Orisha, remember that Oshumare is a very peaceful Orisha who does not like being surrounded by loud noises or feelings of aggression or hostility. Be calm, take off your shoes, sit down and wait for him to appear. Oshumare may appear in the form of bright light, as a reflection in the water, in a mirror, or in any other peaceful setting.

Symbols and Ebbo

Oshumare is associated with the sea, the moon, and the color white. As such, these are the main symbols associated with Oshumare. Some of the most common Ebbo of Oshumare include seashells, pearls, oyster shells, seaweed, white fabrics, and candles. Oshumare can also be offered white rice, egg whites, white bread, white flowers, coconut, and water.

Olokun

Olokun is the Orisha of wealth and the ocean. Olokun is a fierce spirit living in the ocean and is also associated with the color white. Olokun can also be considered an androgynous spirit who can be both male and female depending on the situation. While on earth, this deity takes the male form. Olokun is a greedy spirit who must be appeased with offerings and sacrifices. Wealth, greed, and ferocity are their most prominent characteristics. They are the source of all riches, which they can give to anyone who appeases them during the ritual. Colored blue and white, they are deep and mysterious, like the seas and lakes they rule over.

How to Greet Olokun

If you are interested in Olokun, you can offer white items or white flowers as a gift. Olokun is also associated with white foods such as rice and salt. Offers need to be in abundance and practiced near the sea or ocean. You can also offer them a white candle during your invocation.

Symbols and Ebbo

The symbols of Olokun are their purity and the color white. Olokun can be associated with the number three. The Ebbo of Olokun is salt and a white flower.

Oshosi (Oshoshi)

In addition to being known as the master of the forest, Oshisi is the god of fortune and prophecy. Oshosi may have originated in the Yoruba people of southwestern Nigeria, where he is the chief Orisha of the forests, hunting, and war. In south-eastern Nigeria, Oshosi is a very popular Orisha. There are many festivals in which he is celebrated and worshipped. One of these festivals is Oshogbo, which takes place between the months of July and August. As well as being the Orisha of the hunt, he is also associated with killing animals for food. Since he is a food provider, he is strongly associated with farmers, families, and wealth. Oshosi is a fierce warrior and is the patron of fighting and sports, making him aggressive in nature.

How to Greet Oshosi

You can greet Oshosi by lighting a candle or incense in the forest or woods. If you seek prosperity, you can offer him something sweet, like honey or flowers. Oshosi is the god of the forest, so he will be pleased to see a tree inside his shrine. Another way to greet Oshosi is to offer him food, such as a goat's head or a roasted pig.

Oshosi Symbols and Ebbo

The animal's blood is needed for Oshosi's rituals, together with honey and mahogany leaves.

Oshosi's main colors are white, yellow, and blue. Oshosi's main symbol is the tiger, representing his ferocity and strength. His Ebbo mahogany bark or leaves, honey, and gold coins.

These are just a few examples of spirits from the Yoruba traditions. Many other spirits and deities from these cultures are just as interesting and powerful. But the White Orisha is a spirit of healing and purity. Any one of these deities can help bring light and positivity into your world. They are also a spirit of service and can help you to serve others in your life.

Now that you know who some of the White Orisha are and what they represent, remember that no Orisha is better than another. All Orisha represent different aspects of life and have different gifts to share. So when choosing one, find the one that best suits your personality and needs. Once you have done this, you can start observing Orisha's energy and learn more about what they can offer you.

Chapter 5: The Red and Black Orishas

The Orisha faith is one of the oldest religions in the world, with roots that reach back to 400 BCE. Over the course of history, this unique and diverse faith has spread to many different regions and has been practiced by many people. Its popularity has spread throughout Cuba (Santeria), Haiti (Voodoo), Brazil (Candomble), and Nigeria (Yoruba). The deities of this faith are constantly evolving to incorporate new beliefs and deities. The Orisha Osanyin and Orisha Shango are two Orishas gods of passion, and each has a distinct personality and role within the faith. Their followers often wear different colors, including the more virtuous white discussed in the previous chapter.

The Orisha faith is one of the oldest religions in the world, with roots that reach back to 400 BCE.

Rept0n1x, CC BY-SA 3.0 <https://creativecommons.org/licenses/by-sa/3.0>, via Wikimedia Commons: https://commons.wikimedia.org/wiki/File:Shango_staff,_oshe_Shango,_World_Museum_Liverpool.JPG

Just like their lighter counterparts, these Orishas can be seen as forces of nature, spirits, or incarnations of natural energies. This chapter will explore the origins of this category of Orisha and its connection to the Yoruba religion. The Orishas are usually known as the Red and Black Orishas, as their primary colors are red and black. They often manifest as complex or compound deities with distinct personalities and unique characteristics. Each deity represents a specific element, force, or natural phenomenon. These entities can be found in almost all Afro-American religions in one form or another. They are often referred to as spirits, gods, saints, angels, devas, or totems. They have different roles but serve the same purpose: bringing balance back into our lives so we can live a healthy and happy life.

Main Characteristics of the Red and Black Orishas

Understanding the Orisha categories is crucial. While each Orisha has its own personality, some are more wrathful than others. But despite their tendency to anger easily, they also have a positive side to them. They can help you solve problems in your life if you work with them in the right way. These Orishas represent the energy of new beginnings and passion for life. They help followers embrace change, release anger and fear, and find their inner strength during difficult times. They all have their own distinct characteristics, rituals, and origin stories. Red Orishas are spirits that were born from fire and light, while black Orishas come from darkness and water. The color red is used to describe these deities because red is associated with blood and life flow. This indicates that red Orishas are associated with healing and protection. Similarly, black Orishas are connected to witchcraft, sorcery, and the dark arts. Most deities in this category have fiery temperaments, are war-like, and are aggressive with their power. Understanding the different Orishas can help you determine what type of assistance you need from the divine.

Ogun

Ogun is the Yoruba Orisha of iron and the lightning bolt. Ogun is considered to be a warrior god, and he represents strength, power, and fearlessness. He is also associated with the color black and death. However, Ogun is not evil; he simply represents the power of death and destruction. In Africa, Ogun is often seen as the opposite of Yemaya, an Orisha who protects and gives life. As well as being the protector of iron, Ogun is also linked with thunderstorms. This connection makes him an ideal protector of crops in areas where thunderstorms are common. In Trinidad, Ogun is believed to be a messenger between the dead and the living. He is also responsible for bringing lightning bolts down from the sky to show that someone has died or been struck by lightning. Ogun's pivotal role is as a judge. He determines what happens to people after they die by weighing their sins against their virtues and deciding if their souls deserve eternal punishment or eternal reward. Black and red are sacred colors for Ogun because they represent both his destructive abilities and his heavenly quality of protecting those who need them most.

How to Greet Ogun

To honor Ogun properly, always show respect for all life and nature, both on your own behalf and on behalf of those that you love. Take two steps back from the Orisha and bow low. Raise your right hand and say, "Mo w nibi" (I am here). Then take one step forward and bow again. After this, you should place a small offering on the ground next to you.

Symbols and Ebbo

Like all Orisha, he has many symbols that can be used to represent him. One of the most common is iron, which represents strength, power, and protection. It can also be used to represent money, success, and victory. As an Ebbo for Orgun, worshipers mark symbols onto clay or wood, or they can be either painted or stitched onto clothing. Symbols such as an axe, spear, or shield relate to his powers, and are used to pay homage to his ability to protect and heal.

Esu (Eshu)

Esu closely resembles the mythical Aztec god Huitzilopochtli. Since these cultures existed at different times, historians believe that Esu was a shared deity between the African and Latin American regions. The similarities between these depictions and rituals lead many experts to believe that Esu is one of the oldest and most influential red Orishas within African spirituality. This deity is an intermediary between humans and the supreme being known as Olodumare. In Orisha cultures, Esu is the god responsible for regulating disease and death. As such, he is often shown as a skeletal figure who wears a crown made of human bones. Esu is often accompanied by a dog and a horse and is associated with red and black. This helps people understand his role as a deity who controls the spread of disease through animals. Esu is also depicted as a bird who has the ability to travel between the spiritual and physical worlds. This has helped inspire legends that describe Esu as a mythical creature with strong magical abilities. Esu can help people struggling with health issues, disease, or addiction. He also serves as a guide who helps people transition smoothly through the different stages of life.

How to Greet Esu

People who wish to greet this deity should start by facing south. Next, they should say "Babalu Aye Esu" three times and then bow three times. When you feel the need for protection against health issues or death, you may perform this ritual during the San Lazaro ritual, or at any other time you feel the need for such protection.

Symbols and Ebbo

Ritual foods that can be offered to Esu include palm oil, beans, cornmeal, popcorn, and farofa, a flour made from manioc. Four-legged birds and animals are also offered as Ebbo sacrifices. Other artifacts used in his greeting rituals include a broom, a needle, and a knife. The broom is a symbol that is used to cleanse the spirits of the dead out of homes. The needle and knife are used during ritualistic cutting that can help heal and protect individuals from disease.

Babalu-Aye

Orisa Babalu-Aye is a black Orisha associated with witchcraft, sorcery, and the dark arts. This deity is often depicted as a shadowy figure who uses his powers to manipulate and harm people and is often accompanied by a dog and a rooster. This helps people understand his role as a deity who uses witchcraft to spread pain and suffering but also healing. Babalu-Aye is also associated with the number nine and the colors black, purple, and yellow. He promotes cures for illnesses and healing for those who are close to death, but some believe him to be capable of bringing disease to humans. Babalu-Aye is most commonly worshiped by those who believe they have been given bad luck or misfortune in their lives. He is also invoked when someone's life is about to end, especially if it happens unexpectedly. His other purpose is to help people make their own decisions rather than having them made for them by others.

How to Greet Babalu-Aye

When greeting Babalu Aye, you should stand with your hands in your pockets, with your head slightly tilted towards the ground. This shows respect and humility towards this deity. You should also avoid saying words like "no," "don't," or "stop," as they can offend this deity. Next, you should say "Alápa-dúpé," meaning "One who kills and is thanked for it." This ritual can be performed at any time when you want to tap into Babalu-Aye's witchcraft powers. On the day of celebration for this Orisha, people visit the ocean or a river to cleanse themselves of negative energies.

Symbols and Ebbo

Offerings are also made to this deity appealing for help in healing loved ones. Babalu Aye is associated with the number seven. This number is considered lucky and is often used in amulets and jewelry to protect those who wear them. The symbols of the Orisha Babalu Aye are the snake, a bowl of herbs, and the number seven. The Ebbo of this Orisha is tobacco and water.

Osanyin

Osanyin is one of the most mysterious Orishas. He is not well known outside of the Yoruba people, and even within the community, his worshipers are hard to find. Osanyin is the god associated with plants, healing, medicine, vegetation, and the harvest, which makes him an essential part of the Orisha faith. Osanyin means 'the hunter' in Yoruba. Originally, he was a hunter, and it was through the experiences he had in the forest that he became an Orisha. He is also associated with healing. As a result, Osanyin is often illustrated with medicinal plants, leaves, and herbs in his clothing. His colors are red, green, and black. Red represents passion and creativity, while black is associated with transformation. And green because of his role in providing food and his deep connection with nature. He is often seen as a deity of fertility. Various saints' feast days can be related to celebrating his significance. These celebrations relate particularly to Saint Joseph and his Americanized syncretism. These days, people make offerings to their plants and trees, appealing for strong and healthy growth. Osanyin is a hunter who prefers a solitary life away from large groups of people. But he is revered for his ability to see through deception or lies and to expose those who are hiding secrets.

How to Greet Osanyin

There is nothing to worry about when getting in touch with Osanyin because he has a patient personality, but he can be very stern if he feels someone has misused his powers or if he sees his followers doing harm to others. He is very intelligent and can solve any problem with careful thought. Besides being practical, he is also playful. He is most often receptive to single people, both male and female, and the elderly due to his desire to protect those who might feel vulnerable. When greeting the Osanyin, you must be humble, respectful, and kind. Men should wear blue clothing, whereas women should wear a blue headscarf or blue jewelry. Many people also like to use blue flowers when worshiping Osanyin. To show your respect, you should kneel on the ground and bow your head before you speak to him.

Symbols and Ebbo

There is no fixed understanding of these symbols when it comes to Osanyin and his worship. The interpretation of his attributes and significance can vary among different groups of followers and may also differ depending on where they live. But some of the common symbols for Osanyin are the drum, horse, leaves, and birds, as is a green hand, which is called an Odu Ifa. This symbol represents his role as a healer and his connection with nature. The Ebbo for Osanyin is cassava bread, palm wine, and pepper.

Shango

According to Shango folklore, he was born into slavery but rose up against his master in an attempt to gain freedom. Shango was first worshiped by the Yoruba people of West Africa, and today, he is one of the most popular Orishas among practitioners of Santeria. Shango is considered a very temperamental deity. He is known to have a quick temper, but he is also quick to forgive those who are sincere in their apologies. He is also quick-witted and a natural leader who knows how to get things done efficiently. He is fearless and takes risks. He is also very generous and loving, which makes him a compassionate deity. He is also known for being a great healer who uses his powers for good. Because he is associated with thunder and lightning, he is often depicted with lightning bolts or a sword as his emblem. Associated with the colors red and white, this deity of fire and passion represents life flowing through all living things. Often associated with fertility and new beginnings, this Orisha is commonly depicted as a large bearded man carrying a sword or a staff. As a war deity that symbolizes strength and power, he brings change, transformation, and a new order. On the day of Shango's celebration, people clean their houses and make offerings to their ancestors.

How to Greet Shango

Shango is a non-physical god who can be invoked by anyone who sincerely desires to connect with him. Shango's purpose is to protect people from evil spirits, and he is said to have a very long reach. Therefore, worshipers need to show respect when greeting him by bowing down and making offerings such as food or drinks.

The best time to greet Shango is at dawn when the first rays of sunlight are starting to peek over the horizon. If you cannot greet him at this time, you can do so any time after sunset until midnight - just make sure you are respectful when doing so.

Symbols and Ebbo

If you wish to pray to Shango, you should carry objects representing his symbols, such as items connected to lightning bolts, thunderbolts, and storm clouds. You can also wear a representation of one of his symbols, such as a feathered costume or a helmet adorned with horns. When praying to Shango, ensure you are respectful of others around you. You should also keep your thoughts positive so that Shango can help you achieve your goals.

Ebbo is a small bottle of rum used in voodoo rituals, usually filled with rum, herbs, or other ingredients.

Oya

Oya is from a class of deities in the Yoruban and Afro-Caribbean religions. In the Yoruba religion, she is one of the hottest-tempered deities, married to Shango. In other cultures, including Haitian Vodou and Candomblé, she is known as Iansã. In Yoruba, Oya takes the role of the goddess of fresh water and is associated with spring water and wells. She takes on different roles in other cultures, such as healing, fertility, and wisdom. Oya's image shows her as a young woman wearing a headdress with two horns that resemble those of a cow or calf. She also holds plants and animals in her hands to symbolize her ability to heal and protect nature.

Some depictions have her holding a pitcher full of water to symbolize her role as the giver of fresh drinking water for humans and animals alike. Some statues show Oya pouring water from one container to another to demonstrate her ability to move from place to place without ever getting tired. At times, Oya can be fierce, protecting people from storms and floods, but she can also be nurturing and protective when needed. As Orisha of childbirth, Oya also provides guidance for pregnant women and new mothers.

How to Greet Oya

To greet Oya, you'll need to first ground yourself by walking or sitting in silence for a few minutes. To be prosperous and abundant in all areas of your life in the future, you'll need to ask Oya to remove all obstacles in your way. Afterward, it's time to offer food, drink, or money as a form of thanks.

Symbols and Ebbo

A significant aspect of Oya's worship needs to be understood: she cannot be bargained with or bargained out of. This means that if you want something from Oya, you must offer something of equal value in return. She is called the "mother of nine," which comes from her nine stillborn children. Plants and trees often grow from mounds of earth, so when given over as offerings, Oya interprets them as giving life to the world. In addition to Ebbo and images, there are also ritual items for use in worshiping Oya, such as paper money, shells, candles, and tobacco leaves. The Oya Ebbo is a special offering given at all times of the year to the Orisha, who is believed to be present everywhere all the time. It includes food, drink, and other items that symbolize life and nature, such as growing plants or blood.

Different cultures have adapted and adopted religions throughout the world to fit their unique lifestyles. A prime example of this is the Orisha faith of African spirituality, which blends ancestral traditions with new beliefs. The Orisha faith has a diverse group of deities known as the Orishas. As a result, there are many variations in how these deities are worshiped and what they represent. These deities are seen as intermediaries between humans and the supreme being. Each Orisha provides a specific type of assistance to help people cope with everyday struggles or deal with stressors in their lives.

These deities represent natural forces, human principles, instincts, or even different aspects of human personality. They are manifestations of the Supreme Creator and intermediaries between mankind and the divine. In essence, Orishas are messengers from God to humanity. As we go about our daily lives, they provide us with guidance and help us make sense of our existence on this planet by teaching us about love, faithfulness, sacrifice, and other passionate aspects of life. Some of these might be confusing for us at times but nonetheless are essential to understanding human nature.

Chapter 6: The Orisha and Ancestor Altar Setup

In this chapter, you'll find all you need to know about setting up an altar when you want to contact your Orishas. You'll get practical instructions, including where to best place your altar, what to use for decoration, and how to cleanse, maintain, and more. However, before you dive into all this, you'll read about the benefits of having this sacred place and whether or not it's necessary to do it in the first place.

Some practitioners swear that altars provide lots of opportunities to develop their practice.
Mauro Didier, CC0, via Wikimedia Commons:
https://commons.wikimedia.org/wiki/File:Un_autel_de_santeria_d%C3%A9di%C3%A9_%C3%A0_Oshun,_orisha_de_l%27amour_CUBA._TRINIDAD_culte_de_Santeria_._Autel_d%27Oshun.jpg

Advantages and Disadvantages of Setting Up an Altar

You might wonder whether or not you need to set up an altar for your spiritual practices. Some practitioners swear that altars provide lots of opportunities to develop their practice, while others skip this step because they don't need a dedicated altar. So, to answer this question, it really depends on what feels right for you. There are pros and cons to building an altar to honor your ancestors or spiritual guides.

One of the things about having an altar is that it helps you focus your energy and get closer to your ancestors or the Orishas. However, depending on the strength of your spirituality, you may not need to have an altar for this. If you have a strong intuition and can focus your energy and intention during your worship time without the need for anything special, you probably won't want an altar. And if you are highly creative, you'll be able to perform acts of spiritual practice from anywhere. For some people, decorating an altar is a way of expressing their artistic abilities and helps them communicate their ideas, beliefs, and emotions.

For those who prefer practical solutions, decorating the altar for a particular purpose (like honoring the Orishas and ancestors or asking them for guidance and protection) is just too time-consuming. For example, in the case of an altar for Orishas, you'll need to take the time to learn their symbolism and corresponding associations. Otherwise, you won't be able to adorn your altar correctly to communicate with these ancient divinities. And if you aren't skilled at crafts, you'll probably have to buy most of the decorations, which can also be costly. You may be focused on spiritual development and not on communication. Or you may not spend too much time in front of an altar. In either case, you probably won't need to invest that much time, money, or energy in creating a dedicated space for your practice.

When it comes to space, not having enough of it is one of the most common reasons for people not creating an altar. The number of people living in urban settings turning to unorganized religions is growing quickly. Living in a small, rented apartment often doesn't leave enough space for dedicated altars, especially if you aren't living alone. You can always sneak a few symbols and items onto your nightstand, but that kind of defeats the purpose of having a sacred space. Everything you place on an altar should be placed there intentionally. Putting or leaving random objects on your altar can mean that you may not get the results you want from your practices.

People who are used to being part of a large religious community often set up an altar to keep feeling like they belong. Building an altar will be the best option if you feel the need for centering and grounding during your practices. Having this space will allow you to learn more about symbols. After all, you'll need to keep most of them in your head if your altar has to double up as something else and you have to decorate and redecorate it. For example, the Orishas all have different symbols and offerings. So, unless you're working with only one (some choose to work only with the Supreme god), you'll need to change your symbolism for each one.

Another good reason for making an altar is to redirect negative influences in your life to positive actions. For example, simply building a space where you'll be able to connect with your guide can allay your fears of being influenced by evil or dark forces. Then again, you may choose to brush off this influence by simply implementing other healthy habits into your life.

Some say that building an altar is relaxing and helps them break away from the stress of everyday life. It's also said to be inspiring. Yet others claim that it's not as motivating as having the magical energy permeate every corner of your home. And if you choose not to have an altar and practice your craft wherever it's more convenient for you, you'll be able to do just that. Eventually, you'll have cleaned and filled every part of your home with good spiritual energy. Every place you go to will help you stay calm and keep you wanting to grow spiritually and improve your practice.

As you can see, there is a positive side to creating an altar and not setting one up. How you choose to organize your practice will be up to you. If you opt to build an altar for your ancestors or the Orishas, you can learn how to do it in the continuation of this chapter.

Creating an Orisha Altar

Before you decide to set up an altar for an Orisha, choose an appropriate place for it. Where you put your altar depends on several factors, including your personal preferences, whether you practice alone or with a group, and how much space you have for it. For example, if you're a private person and practice alone, having an altar in your bedroom will give you all the privacy you need. And if you have a small space, you'll want to keep your altar hidden away from doorways and windows, which can be sources of negative energy. On the other hand, if you're setting an altar where an entire family or household will practice, it makes more sense to do so in the living room or a room all members frequent. Once you've chosen the place for your altar, you'll need to cleanse the entire space. Smudging is one of the most common practices for clearing out negative energy. You can also choose purifying incense, a cleansing spell, or literally sweeping the place clean. The latter is recommended even if you opt for smudging because clutter and dirt attract negative energy, and you'll want to keep this away from your altar. Before cleansing a space, open your windows to let the negative energy out and positive vibes flow into your space. Depending on how you want to do it, you can recite prayers during the cleansing or put on some relaxing music if you like. Make sure that the altar itself is already in the room when you're doing the cleansing. That way, you won't have to repeat the process.

You don't need to buy a specific piece of furniture for your altar. You can work on whatever you have with the largest flat surface. Tabletops are usually the best option, but old dressers or nightstands work just as well. Just don't keep anything in them that's unrelated to the altar's purpose. You can also use your floor if you don't have another surface to work on - you'll put a cloth on your altar anyway, so it doesn't matter.

After cleansing the space, you may put the base of your altar into place. If you're using an item that was already in the room, you can skip this step. You can move on to selecting what you want to put on the altar. This depends on your purpose, so make sure you work out which Orisha you want to honor and start collecting the symbolic items needed. As you remember from the previous chapters, each Orisha has its preferences for offerings. Consult the respective chapters for the correct Orisha and symbol correspondences. Whichever Orisha you choose to honor, ensure that whatever you place on the altar matches the Orisha perfectly, as some items may be taboo for some of the divinities. Some of the items to include on your Orisha-dedicated altar are:

- A cloth in the color associated with the Orisha you're working with
- Symbol of the Orisha
- The representation of the four elements through candles, crystals, etc.
- Larger candles that burn for several days
- Offerings for the Orisha
- Incense (optional)
- Spell work, ritual tools (optional)

Place the symbol of the Orisha right in the center of your altar. If you're making an offering, you may place it in front of the symbol. The pictures or representations of the four elements should be placed around the surface's edge at equal distances from each other and the center. Any other items you choose should be set according to the intent of their use. Take each of them into your hands, and let your intuition decide where you should place them.

Altars need to be cleansed after each use, especially if you've used them for spiritual communication. Sometimes messages can pick up negative energy on their way to and from the gods. If you don't cleanse the altar and your space after working on it, you should do it before you use them again. You can do it the way you did before setting up an altar, or you can choose another method; it's entirely up to you.

You might also want to create a ritual that lets you use the energy of your sacred space all the time. Whether it's through prayer, journaling, meditation, yoga, or any other method, the best way to take advantage of your altar is to stay connected to it.

Creating an Ancestor Altar

Before reaching out to the divinities, set up an altar for your ancestors as well. After all, their energy should be easily available to you to harness. This will also make it easier for you to develop this practice. It can help you lay the foundation for reaching a higher level of spiritual energy, such as the power of the Orishas. Apart from being the source of wisdom, your ancestors can also act as protectors, healers, and guides on your life's journey. They can facilitate decision-making in and out of magical practices. Ancestor altars are personal representations of your connection to the spirituality of those who lived before you. Through them, you can build a line of communication with your ancestors, which is especially important if you don't know them personally. Because, in this case, you won't know whether they'll help you before talking to them.

The initial steps of the preparation process (cleansing, finding the best place, and setting up the altar) are the same as with an Orisha altar. You may refer to how it was described in the previous section. After completing them, you should decide which ancestors you want to work with and which ones you would rather not welcome at your altar. Setting up pictures or items that used to belong to them should help signal to them who is welcome, but you may want to reiterate this with a quick spell. You can also recite the names of those whom you wish to exclude.

If you haven't had any personal connection with your ancestors, don't worry. While having a picture or personal items helps, you may choose to represent them otherwise. Do a little research on them through your living relatives and add items you know they've cherished. If you used to know the ancestors you'd be working with, you should include objects reminding you of your time with them. This can be a meal you had together, a game you played, or a picture of a place where you've created memories with them. This will help revive the connection that's often lost when a soul passes on and leaves the world of the living.

You should also make tools for protecting yourself from disruptive spirits. Not all of them will listen when you list them as excluded and will try to contact you anyway. If you feel as if a bad spirit is still around after your session, don't use your altar until you've thoroughly cleaned it.

Apart from reaching out to your blood relatives, altars can also be used to communicate with historical figures you've found inspiring and whose wisdom you feel can improve your life. Contacting a chosen mentor or teacher is also a possibility, and it also contributes to spiritual growth.

Here are some items to place on your ancestral altar:
- **A Cloth:** White is preferred by many, but you can also use a cloth in your ancestor's favorite color, just as you do with the Orishas. If you need your ancestors' help with healing, you can use colors associated with the organ you're having problems with. Or, you can simply use a piece of fabric that has a personal meaning for you.
- **A Glass of Water:** This is recommended for added protection but can also serve as a tool to harness and channel natural energy.
- **A Symbol of Your Ancestor or Spiritual Guide:** If the spirit is unrelated to you. You can invite anyone you identify with, even if you need healing from a personal or family trauma.
- **Candles:** Depending on your experience level, establishing communication may take some time. So, for starters, it's a good idea to get 7-day candles. These are great to re-light if you have to stop what you're doing to tend to your everyday activities or sleep before going back to spiritual communication. They are also larger, which makes them a better choice than tea lights. Ideally, the candles should be your only source of light as you'll use them to attract the ancestral spirit. Yet another reason you should get larger ones.
- **Offerings:** This is optional, but if you need more extensive help, your ancestors will definitely appreciate the gesture of being offered food and drink. Particularly if it's their favorite selection. The offerings symbolize their soul's nourishment and help attract the spirit to your sacred space.
- **The Symbols of the Four Elements**
- **The Intention You Want to Manifest:** This is also optional. If you don't feel the need to write down your intention and place it on the altar, you don't have to. However, beginners find it easier to keep their minds focused on their intention when they have it written down in front of them.

Before you set up the altar, you must reflect on your reasons for doing it. While this reflection period may also be included before creating an Orisha altar, it's even more necessary when you're trying to reach ancestral spirits. Since you'll be communicating with people you've had a connection with (even if it's only on a spiritual level), your personal reasons truly matter. And not just for achieving your goal. If you don't understand why you're doing something during the setup process or you're doing something that isn't in line with your values, it probably won't help you make a meaningful connection.

The best way to set up an altar for your ancestors is to simply listen to your gut. This is the source of the spiritual energy you'll use to make a connection with your ancestors. Besides, your ancestors and you likely shared common values. If your gut tells you that creating an altar in a certain way is a good idea, your ancestors' intuition would have probably told them the same thing. If they would have liked you to set up, you're already a step closer to spiritual growth.

Chapter 7: African Magical Practices

African magic has a nefarious reputation, especially through the media and Hollywood's lens of it. People may have the misconception that African magic, also known as Hoodoo, is dark and evil. Some even refer to it as black magic.

Magic is just like any other tool; it can be used for both good and evil.
https://pixabay.com/es/photos/mu%c3%b1ecos-vud%c3%ba-mu%c3%b1ecas-brujer%c3%ada-vud%c3%ba-3380821/

The vast majority either view magic as fake or evil. However, there are some people who are aware of magic's existence in the world. They know its power and, more importantly, view it as a neutral tool.

At the end of the day, magic is just like any other tool. It can be used for both good and evil. African magic is no different from any kind of magic practice or any other tool for that matter.

In this chapter, you'll be exposed to Hoodoo in greater depth and learn about natural ingredients you can use in your craft. You'll also learn how and when to use these ingredients to help you with your activities.

Voodoo, Hoodoo, Conjure-Work, and Rootwork

People often confuse Voodoo, or Vodou, with Hoodoo. As you may know by now, Vodou is a religious faith that is practiced by Haitians, Caribbeans, and some Africans in West Africa. Hoodoo, on the other hand, is a spiritual and magical practice. It is practiced by many Africans, including African Americans from New Orleans.

Both Vodou and Hoodoo Are African spiritual practices. This means they are closed practices, and only Africans can use them. Some minor Voodoo and Hoodoo practitioners welcome outsiders into their indigenous practices, but they have to undergo an initiation process. This is considered rare, so not every outsider can count on entering this world.

Being referred to as closed practices means they are related to indigenous people. African countries and their people were colonized for centuries. Africans held tightly to their spiritual beliefs when they were fighting off colonizers and being held captive. During these terrifying times, Voodoo believers prayed to the divine lwa while Hoodoo practitioners practiced their rootwork to free themselves and their people.

So what are conjure-work and rootwork exactly? The word conjure is used interchangeably with Hoodoo. These two words signify the same thing, African magic. The word conjure is self-explanatory since it implies working with a spirit. Hoodoo relies on working with spirits of the earth, air, water, sky, and different Lwas. There are spirits all around us, and Hoodoo comes in contact with them.

The spirits are seen as creative and mischievous. Some spirits will help you or guide you. Others are malevolent and carry evil energies. Usually, in Hoodoo, practitioners work with helpful spirits who will assist the conjurer.

In the Hoodoo realm, the word rootwork is often used. This word refers to every part of the plant, not just its roots. This means that a practitioner may use the petals, stems, leaves, seeds, and roots.

Today, Africans remember their ancestors' bravery and endurance, so they practice these beliefs to honor their ancestors and express gratitude. Moreover, Hoodoo is more of a way of life for any practitioner. This is why it is inappropriate when an outsider practices either of these spiritual faiths without an initiation process.

Whether you are here as a native practitioner, an initiate, or a curious person, there is a lot to learn about Hoodoo and its numerous rituals, magical spells, and recipes.

Oil Magic

In Hoodoo magic, oils are seen as a medium of transportation that facilitates the spirit's journey from its realm to this one. Oils also have numerous properties, but mainly they are used to bring spirits in to help activate the spell. You can use as many oils as you like, so long as they match the spell. Hoodoo practitioners usually create their oil mixtures and store them.

There are various uses for oils. You can work it into candle magic and anoint your candle with it. You can also use your oils for baths or apply them to certain body parts. There are oils that are placed in specific areas in your house for cleansing and protection.

Magical Oil Recipes

Money Oil

This oil's purpose is to draw more money into your life. You can use it to manifest creating more money or receiving more money through your business. It is also used to free oneself from debt. It can help you get money back from family members or anyone who has taken your money and is not giving it back. You can use this oil with candle magic or rituals. To make it, you need the following:

- 1 tiny bottle
- 4 drops of Vanilla
- 1 drop of Vetiver

Love Oil

This recipe contains ingredients that target romantic love, so do not use it for platonic relationships. You can use this oil to attract someone into your life. For this to work, the person you are attracting should be a person of interest to you. This oil mixture can be used with candle magic. To create this recipe, you'll need the following:

- 1 bottle
- 1 tsp of grapeseed carrier oil
- 6 drops of rose essential oil
- 1 drop of ginger essential oil
- 5 drops of patchouli essential oil
- A pinch of dried ginger root
- A pinch of dried patchouli
- A pinch of rose petals

Break Spells and Banish Bad Luck

This oil recipe is used to free yourself from a spell, bad luck, jinxes, and black magic. It is best that you create this recipe and keep it at your house. You'll know if you are experiencing a negative impact of a spell when you do not feel like yourself, lose sleep, and feel drained and tired. This mixture will require the following:

- 1 jar
- Sunflower oil
- Poke root
- Rule Sandalwood

You can come up with your own measurements for this recipe. When you are done with this recipe, leave it out in the sun for a month. You can anoint yourself with this oil when it is ready to be used.

Dip your finger in the oil and trace the cross symbol above your brows, heart, hands, and feet. Make sure that you follow this order. You may anoint your private parts if the spell includes your sexual energy. If you anoint your private parts, then make sure you do so before you mark your feet. When you are done, trace the cross on the back of your neck.

When you have finished, walk away until you reach the edge of your property or a crossroads. Do not look back when you are walking away. When you reach your property line, shake off your misfortune. You can visualize yourself being relieved of everything that has been holding you back. This recipe is used with Voodoo dolls and gris-gris, which you'll read about in the coming chapter.

Banish Obstacles

- Small skeleton key
- 10 drops of fresh orange juice
- Scraped bits of dried orange peel
- 2 drops of orange food color
- 10 drops of fresh lemon juice
- Scraped bits of dried lemon peel

Protection and Cleansing

This oil mixture recipe is used to cleanse yourself or your space from unwanted energies. This mixture is also used to cure oneself of illnesses and eliminate bad energy. It is also used to ward off evil energy. To create this mixture, you'll need the following:

- 1 bottle
- 5 drops of rosemary essential oil
- 15 drops of lemon essential oil
- 20 drops of clove essential oil
- 10 drops of eucalyptus essential oil
- 10 drops of cinnamon essential oil
- Add black salt (optional)

You may add black salt if you are creating this mixture to cleanse your house. However, if you want to bathe with this mixture, then do not use black salt.

Candles

Candle magic is known relatively well and is practiced in different spiritual beliefs. Hoodooists also practice candle magic in their own way. Hoodoo practitioners believe that candles are light threads that connect them to the creator, spirits, and supernatural forces.

Candles are connected with protection, restoring balance and justice, wealth, good luck, love, and health. Hoodoo has assigned certain candle colors with certain intentions. The idea is that specific candle colors vibrate with certain concepts.

Candle Colors

- **White**

White candles are associated with purity and healing. This means you can purify a place or energy using a white candle. You can also use it to heal yourself mentally or spiritually.

- **Yellow**

Yellow candles have various functions. You can use them to have your prayers answered. For instance, it would be a good idea to use a yellow candle when you are waiting for a sign or confirmation that your prayers were heard and about to be answered. You can also use them when you want to lure attraction into your life. These candles are also used when you are dealing with a friendship issue. You may want to attract good friends in your life or have a problem with one of your friends.

- **Orange**

Orange candles are mainly used when you are curious or anxious about the future. Let's say that you were following a fixed plan, but for some reason, it was interrupted. You can find out what the future holds for you now through an orange candle.

- **Pink**

Pink candles are mainly used for romantic relationships. Whether you are attracting romance to your life or maintaining a romantic relationship, they are also used for beauty and allure.

- **Red**

Red candles are similar to pink ones as they are associated with romance. They are also used for love on a broader level. You can use them to manifest love into your life, which is not necessarily romantic love. You can manifest love from others or sustain self-love. They are also used to bring in good health and passion.

- **Brown**

Brown candles are linked to restoration. Brown is associated with soil, earth, and tree bark. Naturally, brown is connected to renewal and revival energy. They are also used to win any kind of legal battle.

- **Purple**

Purple is associated with royalty and power. This is why purple colors are connected to ambition and power. You can use purple to find your own power or if you are seeking powerful placements in the material world.

- **Green**

Similar to brown, green is also associated with nature. You can use it for harvesting or giving your plants powerful positive energy. Green candles are connected with money and wealth, so you can use them to receive more money in life. Green candles are also used to attract good job opportunities.

- **Blue**

Blue candles are used to bring joy and happiness to one's life. They are also used to attract unity and people with good intentions into your life.

- **Black**

Black candles are mainly used for protection. This means that you can use them to shield yourself from negative energies and send unwanted energies back to the sender or the source.

Mixing Candles

You can be very creative with your candle magic. You don't have to stick to one color; you can include multiple candle colors for the same spell. For instance, you can use black and green to break your bad luck streak with money. You can use black and white candles to purify yourself of negative energy and return it back to the sender. You can use black and red to break or shield yourself from a love spell. You can use white and pink to heal your romantic relationships. You can combine as many colors as you like, so long as your spell is clear and makes sense.

How to Cast a Spell with Candles

Now that you know what candle colors correspond to, it is time to learn how to cast a spell. First of all, set your intentions. You need to be clear on what you want in or out of your life. You might have a general idea but feel lost when it comes to casting a spell. This is why it is important to thoroughly consider what you want to attain from your spell.

Once you are clear on what you want from your spell, write it down. Think about the candle colors that correspond with your intentions. Get the right candles and carve your wish on them. Try to come up with a short sentence that reflects your intentions. You can carve anything on your candles. It can be a symbol of one of the Lwas, a number, a name, or a sentence. You can anoint your candle with certain oils and herbs. This is optional, but you should know that herbs and oils strengthen your spell. Make sure to pick the right herbs and oils that vibrate with your intentions, just like the candle color.

Exercise 1

Situation #1: You want to bring in friends with good intentions.

- **Use:** Yellow and Blue candles.
- **Write:** I attract friends who have my best interest at heart.
- **Anoint:** (optional)

Situation #2: You want to attract a powerful position in your career that will grant you a lot of wealth.

- **Use:** Purple and green candles.
- **Write:** I am a (insert powerful position), and I am wealthy.
- **Anoint:** (optional)

Cowrie Shell Divination

There are various things found in nature that can be used as divination tools, and you can add cowrie shells to the options available. These shells have been part of divination ceremonies that date back centuries ago and were first used by Yoruba people in West Africa as divination tools.

The cowrie shells are seen as portals or gates to the spirit world. They are a way to hear from the ancestors. The system is simple; one must ask the ancestors a question, shake and toss the shells, and receive an answer from the ancestors. This divination tool does not give complicated answers; it gives a simple yes or a no.

There are different ways to interpret the shells. There are practitioners who use four shells and others who use 16. This chapter will mainly discuss different ways to interpret readings with four shells.

1. Alfia

The Alfia arrangement is made up of four upright cowries. This is considered to be a very loud "yes." This can be the answer that the practitioner seeks or fears the most; it depends on the question asked. Alfia also tells the interpreter that they are blessed with divine assistance. The practitioner may toss the shells again to see how long this 'yes' will last.

2. Etawa

Etawa has three upright shells and one upside-down shell. This is not a strong "yes," but it points towards a "maybe yes" kind of response. This means that the practitioner should consider other areas or examine different factors before making a decision. The interpreter may throw the shells again to get a clearer response.

3. Ejife

This arrangement has two upright and two upside-down shells. This is also another clear "yes" sign. Ejife is considered the ideal "yes" because there is a perfect balance between the "yes and no" or the light and dark. As an interpreter, you do not need to toss the shells again.

4. Okanran

Okanran has one upright and three upside-down shells. This reads as a clear "no." This reading has a sense of strong opposition because three shells are upside-down. This reading also notifies the reader that they should work on whatever they are asking about because there is more work that should be taking place.

5. Oyekun

Oyekun, or four upside-down shells, read as "no." This is a feared result because it indicates that the reader has negative energies surrounding them. They should seriously consider cleansing and ridding themselves of these negative parasites that are draining them of their energy.

Enhance Psychic Powers 114

There are various ways to enhance your spiritual gifts, and one of these ways is getting yourself into a magical spiritual bath. To do this, you'll need the following:

- Anise Seeds
- Holy Water
- Fluid clothing dye
- Florida Water
- White Flower
- 2 white candles
- Vision Oil:
    - 1 bottle
    - 1-star anise
    - Pinch of cinnamon
    - 1 bay leaf
    - 3 drops of frankincense essential oil
    - Pinch of yarrow
    - Pinch of mugwort

Instructions:

Fill your bathtub with warm water. Grab a mug, add 1 tbsp of anise seeds, and pour boiling water until the cup is filled. Let it sit for 10 minutes, and strain the herbs. Fill a bowl with water and the anise water to it. Add a bit of fluid, clothing dye, and holy water into the bowl. Add Florida water as well.

Now take the flower and place it on top of your third eye. Pray and ask the spirits to guide you and open your eye. When you are done, separate the petals from the stem and place them in the bowl. Place your palms into the bowl and pray that your third eye is cleansed from any blockages.

Place two white candles next to your bathtub and sink into the tub. Now, pour the bowl over your head and recite your prayers again. When you have finished, put a bit of vision oil onto the bottom of your feet.

Magic and Freewill

Dabbling with magic means that you are using your energy and integrating with spirits and nature's divine power. This is serious work that involves powerful power sources. Of course, this is great news because you can bring a lot of joy and fortune into your life. However, with great power comes great responsibility. You must be careful if you are casting spells on other people, specifically manipulating their free will. This is not encouraged, especially if you are a beginner. You need to read more and hear from other practitioners. There is nothing wrong with practicing magic, but be careful and approach with caution.

African magic is a vast realm. You do not have to own much to successfully practice conjure work. You can integrate anything into your craft, so long as it comes from mother nature. You can use any oils and store them in your house for any kind of spells. You can also do the same with candles. Remember that you can get creative with your craft so long as you are using it morally. Speaking of which, it is important that you use this craft if you are part of the culture. As explained, Hoodoo is tightly linked with the Africans' ancestors. So if you are not African or an initiate of the practice, then this practice is not for you. However, if you feel connected to conjure work, then seek conjurers who may be able to help you with your initiation process.

Chapter 8: Gris, Mojo Bags, and Voodoo Dolls

In the previous chapter, you were introduced to some better-known African magical practices, but you cannot be properly introduced to Hoodoo without first learning about gris-gris, mojo bags, and voodoo dolls.

Voodoo dolls are used to channel a person's spirit
Guy Donges, CC BY 2.0 <https://creativecommons.org/licenses/by/2.0>, via Wikimedia Commons: https://commons.wikimedia.org/wiki/File:Voodoo_doll.jpg

These talismans have been around for centuries and are powerful and effective. This is why Hoodoo practitioners use them and often carry either gris-gris or mojo bags everywhere they go.

In this chapter, you'll learn about these three talismans and their origins. You'll learn how to create them and how to use them effectively.

Gris-Gris

People often confuse gris-gris with Mojo bags or use them interchangeably. Both of these bags might be similar in the way they look, but they have different functions.

Originally, the gris-gris bag was used by Africans and Arabs. Its sole purpose was to ward off bad spirits and evil energies. The typical gris-gris bag used to have holy Arabic scripture on it. It is also used to carry stones, coins, herbs, flannel, and feathers. Muslims also used to put sand in it to attract a helpful jinn or spirit to shield them from any evil.

Over the years, non-Muslims were introduced to the gris-gris bag, and it soon became a popular item. As a result, the Arabic writings were removed and replaced with other enchanted writing. Today, the gris-gris bag contains different elements influenced by various cultures and beliefs. There are five main elements that should be included when making your own protection bag.

1. Color
2. Odd numbers between 3-13
3. Contents should match your intention
4. Anoint the bag with essential oils
5. Smudge the bag with your own breath, candle smoke, or incense

Colors

Color symbolism is essential when you are making your bag. As you know by now, every color vibrates with a certain energy. Remember that a gris-gris bag's purpose is to protect you from unwanted happenings. For instance, if you want to protect your health, you might choose brown for longevity and pink for health. You can be creative with the colors *as long as you know what your intention is.*

Here is a list that you can refer to:
- **White:** Purity and peace
- **Gray:** Security, intelligence, and sadness
- **Black:** Death, protection, evil, mysterious objects, people, or events
- **Red:** Passion, energy, love, danger, and anger
- **Gold:** Wealth
- **Silver:** Technology
- **Turquoise:** Protection, healing, envy, spiritual life, and femininity
- **Blue:** Security, masculinity, intelligence, trust, and fear
- **Green:** Fertility, money, and jealousy
- **Yellow:** Happiness, creativity, and instability
- **Orange:** Bravery, Friendliness, confidence, and success.
- **Pink:** Health, compassion, and femininity
- **Purple:** Luxury, spirituality, and moodiness
- **Brown:** Longevity and the outdoors
- **Beige:** flexibility

Gris-Gris Bag Content

Nowadays, people put whatever they need in a gris-gris bag, so it is really up to you. The idea is to include things that you believe will help you. Most often, practitioners put in herbs, symbols, pictures, plants, bones, fabric, keys, hair, or nail clippings. Remember that you are creating this bag to protect yourself from harm, so pick out the objects that will shield you. If you want to include herbs in your bag but do not know which ones to choose, you can refer to this list:

- **Penny Royal:** Removes hexes and curses. Protects travelers on their journeys
- **Mistletoe:** Shields you from nightmares and protects you from harmful spirits. (If you use this herb, then it is best to hang the gris-gris bag over your bedroom door for best results)

- **Black Salt:** Absorbs negative energies
- **Frankincense:** Gets rid of evil spirits
- **Copal Tears Resin:** Purifies your space
- **Mandrake:** Protects your house. Hang over a gate or the doorway
- **Saltpeter:** Reduces men's libido
- **Valerian:** Protects you in your sleep
- **Skull Cap:** Protects your money and increases it. Protects your relationships
- **Spearmint:** Protects children

Gris-Gris Bag Instructions

You do not need much to create a gris-gris bag. Firstly, pick out a piece of fabric or anything from which you can make a satchel. Your bag could be made out of fabric or leather if you want to create a traditional bag. Try to incorporate relevant colors in your bag, so dye your leather or pick a piece of fabric with the right colors.

Spread your fabric and insert relevant content. You can put herbs, seeds, plant parts, odd numbers, pictures, written spells, or anything else that you wish to carry with you. When you are done, fold your bag and tie it up with string or rope.

Now, anoint your bag with protective essential oils like tea tree, peppermint, or sage. You don't have to drown your bag with oil; just lightly dress it. Keep your intentions in mind as you anoint the bag. Finally, smudge the bag with sage smoke, incense, candle smoke, or your breath.

Mojo Bags

Similar to the gris-gris bag, mojo bags also ward off evil. However, that is not their only function. Think of mojo bags as physical manifestations of your desires. In other words, they channel your dreams and carry them into the physical realm. Usually, mojo bags are stitched to the inside of your clothes so that it is close to you and always on your person.

Mojo Bag Samples

Gambling

Ingredients:
- 1 green bag
- 1 lucky charm
- 1 lucky hand root
- 1 silver dime
- Ginger root
- 1 Pyrite stone
- 1 whole nutmeg
- Anoint in Hoytt's Cologne or Frankincense essential oil

Steps:

Spread your green bag and put in the aforementioned ingredients. As you do so, visualize your winnings and try to feel the thrill and excitement of winning. Visualize how your ingredients will help. For instance, the lucky hand root guarantees a good outcome for you. The silver dime is also a lucky charm. The ginger root gives you a lucky streak. The Pyrite stone draws money toward you. Finally, the nutmeg guarantees winning, especially by tossing the dice. When you are done, tie your bag with a rope and a lucky charm. For the final touch, anoint your bag with Hoytt's Cologne or Frankincense essential oil.

Respect in the Workplace

Ingredients:
- 1 purple bag
- Snakeroot
- Jasmine essential oil
- Rosemary essential oil
- Rock root

Steps:

Unfold your purple bag and put the snakeroot and rock root. Mix Jasmine and rosemary essential oils and anoint your bag with them. These two oils are known to boost confidence, which will, in return, help you earn respect professionally and everywhere else. Finally, tie your bag and keep it on your person when you are at work.

How to Create a Mojo Bag

Color is important when picking a bag. So be mindful of the colors you choose. More importantly, pay attention to what you'll put into the bag. Normally, anything can be put into the bag, herbs, oils, trinkets, stones, rocks, sand, crystals, or anything else. As long as the content matches your energy, your mojo bag should work.

Do not forget to anoint your bag when you are done stuffing it with herbs or stones. It is important to anoint your bag with oils or liquids that will help you achieve your desires. Here are different liquids and oil blends that you can use to dress your bag with the magical power of essential oils.

Protection Liquids
- Holy water
- Florida water

Protection Oil Blends
- 1 bottle
- 3 drops of Geranium oil
- 15 drops of Myrrh oil
- 10 ml of Olive oil
- 9 drops of Sandalwood oil

Love Oils
- 1 bottle
- 5 drops of Blue Spruce or Cypress oil
- 10 ml of Coconut oil
- 2 drops of Ginger oil
- 10 drops of Orange oil
- 5 drops of Clary Sage oil
- 2 drops of Nutmeg oil
- 10 drops of Ylang Ylang oil

- 1 drop of Rose oil

Prosperity Oils
- 1 bottle
- Green Aventurine crystals/chips
- 2 ounces of distilled water
- 2 milliliters polysorbate 20
- 15 drops of Spearmint oil
- 15 drops of Peppermint oil
- 10 drops of Ginger oil

Voodoo Dolls

Almost everyone is familiar with Voodoo dolls. The general idea is that Voodoo dolls are used to hurt an individual. This notion is far from the truth, and it paints Voodoo dolls in a bad light. The truth is that Voodoo dolls are used to channel a person's spirit. Through this channel, the practitioner can heal or bring fortune to this person. Also, please note that you can create a Voodoo doll of yourself; they are not only used on other individuals.

To channel an individual's spirit into a Voodoo doll, you'll need a personal item from this person. Usually, these items include but are not limited to hair, nail clippings, blood, teeth, and any form of bodily fluids.

Once the link has been established, the practitioner can begin performing healing sessions. These dolls are usually made from fabric and stuffing. They can also be made from corn husks, tree parts, or tree parts.

Practitioners use colored pins to address something specific in this person's life. So, they might use green to address money or red for love affairs and so on. Speaking of colors, different colors channel various themes with Voodoo dolls. So, be mindful when you are choosing your fabric.

Voodoo Doll Colors

- **White:** Channels purity and positive energy. Spiritual, mental, emotional, and physical healing
- **Black:** Banishes evil spirits and negative energy
- **Red:** Brings power and love. Draws in a love interest
- **Purple:** This color is used to communicate with souls in the spirit realm. It is also used to receive wisdom from the spirit world and navigate the psychic realm.
- **Green:** Draws in professional success and increases fertility.
- **Blue:** This color is used to bring tranquility to said person's life. It is also used to channel love and peace.
- **Yellow:** Brings in confidence and success.

Voodoo Doll Instructions

The best thing to do before making your doll is to gather your ingredients first. This will help you be more focused and organized. You'll require the following:

- Fabric
- Stuffing
- Needle
- Thread
- Picture of the person
- Bodily fluids or hair, nail clippings, etc.

Now that you have gathered your supplies, you can begin creating your doll. Spread out the fabric and cut it into the shape of a doll. Make sure that you have enough fabric so that you have room to stitch it together and stuff it with cotton. Stitch the beginnings and endings of the doll and leave room in the middle to create a hole. Stuff this hole with cotton and bodily fluids, nails, or hair. Stitch the hole and make sure it is secure. You can stitch a picture to the doll or tape it to the doll.

Cleanse your working space and doll with sage. When you are conducting your ritual, make sure that you are in the right mindset.

So, if you are bringing healing energy to the Voodoo doll, make sure that you are grounded, dressed in white, and have incense or sage smoke in the room. Protect the doll from bad energies with a salt circle.

When you are summoning this person's spirit, have candles or oils around you. You can also play the drums or have a drum track around you as you are summoning this person's spirit.

Cleansing

In the spiritual realm, cleansing is a necessary step that must be completed. Whether you are practicing Hoodoo, folk magic, or any kind of magic, you need to cleanse your tools. That said, your Voodoo dolls, gris-gris, and mojo bags need to be energetically cleansed.

Why should you cleanse them? These tools absorb energy and manipulate it. So the amount of energy they consume and deal with means they need to be cleansed so that they can be used again. Using any of these objects without properly cleansing them first is not wise.

Gris-Gris Bags

As mentioned before, these bags are specifically made to ward off evil. This means that they are charged with intense energy to protect you from negative ones. In other words, whatever energy they shield you from, they absorb it. So, your gris-gris bag has absorbed large amounts of negative energy.

If you are in tune with your tools, you'll know when they need to be cleansed or recharged. Other times, you'll feel like it has simply stopped working. In this case, you need to sage your gris-gris bag and anoint it in holy water. If your gris-gris bag works again, then you have done your job. However, if it does not, then this means that it absorbs intense energy, and its content needs to be removed and replaced. You do not need to get rid of the bag itself, but cleansing it is vital. Replace the old content with new ones and reuse your gris-gris bag.

Mojo Bags

There are two types of mojo bags, one that banishes bad energy and one that draws in good energy. This means that these two bags will have to be cleansed differently. Energetically cleaning the mojo bag that protects you from evil will resemble the gris-gris bag cleansing method. If you feel that your mojo bag has absorbed too much, you'll need to bathe it in sea salt and smudge it with sage. These two ingredients are known as powerful tools that banish evil energy and clear the air.

Mojo bags that attract good energy do not need to be intensely cleansed. This means that you can spray it with holy water or use sage oil. You can also cleanse it with sage smoke or incense. You can also get creative and mix sage oil, sea salt, and water together and spay the bag to cleanse it.

Voodoo Dolls

Voodoo dolls carry heavy energy, so they must be properly cleaned. There are many ways to do this, but the best method is to do multiple cleansing rituals to ensure that the doll is properly cleansed. Cover the doll in earth soil, then let it soak in both sunlight and moonlight. When this is done, wash your doll with salt and holy water. For the final touch, put some sandalwood oil in the diffuser and smudge your doll with it. Then smudge the doll with sage smoke. These are a lot of steps. You do not have to do all of them. However, if you feel like it needs to be intensely cleansed, you can go through all these steps just to be sure.

These talismans have been painted in a bad light, especially Voodoo dolls. However, as you can see, you can use them to bring in the good and protect yourself from the bad. It is a natural instinct for humans to feel fear and to want to protect themselves from the seen and unseen. This is why carrying a gris-gris bag with you is vital. It is fairly easy to create, and you can take it with you everywhere you go.

The same applies to mojo bags. Not only do these bags protect you from evil, but they also bring in good fortune to you. If you want to heal someone or yourself, you can use a voodoo doll. Voodoo dolls can channel a person's spirit if created properly. Be mindful when you are creating your talismans, and remember to cleanse them.

Chapter 9: Sacred Rituals, Spells, and Baths

This chapter has a few simple spells, rituals, and baths for people who are just starting out in their African spirituality journey and want to learn more. These practices can offer you protection, guidance, prosperity, and much more. Most of them can also be tailored to suit different needs and preferences, and you can use them as described here or add your own spin by centering them more around your own spiritual values. By using different symbolisms and correspondences, you can invoke a different Orisha - and not just the one described in the particular practice. All you need to do is look up the corresponding associations in the previous chapters, apply them, and you'll be able to obtain the results you need.

These practices can offer you protection, guidance, prosperity, and much more.
https://www.pexels.com/photo/woman-in-black-dress-holding-a-lighted-candle-5435271/

A Candle Ritual for Obatala

Obatala is one of the most commonly invoked divinities in all African spiritual religions. Obatala will help you fend off disruptive forces during your practice or day-to-day life. With this simple ritual using a seven-day candle, you can harness his Ashe and achieve your objective. Make sure to add plenty of white elements to enhance the ritual's purifying nature.

You'll need the following:

- A white, seven-day candle
- A representation of Obatala
- A piece of white fabric or yarn
- A white cloth
- Cascarilla - fresh or dry
- Milk
- Coconut (shavings work best)
- Yams
- Any other white food you want to use

Instructions:

1. Clear your altar of anything you won't need for this ritual. You want to remove every item that can serve as a distraction.
2. Cover the altar with the white cloth and place the white candle in the center. Put a symbol representing Obatala next to or in front of the candle.
3. If you're using fresh cascarilla, tie it in a bunch with a piece of white fabric or yarn.
4. If you're using dry cascarilla, chop the leaves and sprinkle them around the candle. Tie the piece of fabric or yarn around the bottom of the candle before spreading the leaves around it.
5. Prepare the white foods, rice, milk, coconut, yams, and anything else you might be using, in separate containers. Place them on the altar in front of the candle and the symbol.

6. Take a few moments to relax, then light the candle, close your eyes, and call on Obatala by reciting the following spell:

"I call on you, Obatala, asking you to please lend me your divine power,

Empower me with patience and wisdom.

I wish to be strong and wise,

So my soul can pursue its destiny.

May I stay compassionate and caring,

And following your example, treat others with great integrity."

Traditionally, the candle is meant to be left burning for seven days and nights. However, this is not recommended because of safety issues and because it's impossible to focus on any spell for that long. Instead, you should choose to burn the candle for regular periods of time over the course of seven days. Whenever you have a little time to work on this during the day, light the candle, and recite the spell. When you are finished, extinguish it until you have time to relight it again. The food should ideally be served raw, but you can also cook them into all-white meals and put some aside for the offering.

Oshun's Nurturing Ritual

Oshun is known for being kind and caring, and she may bring you fertility and plenty in many other areas of your life, like art and work. The goddess can also provide protection and even help cultivate relationships. Tools can include the sunflower and pumpkin, and the color of the tools used in the ritual are all associated with her power.

You'll need the following:

- A representation of Oshun
- 1 pumpkin
- Sunflowers, fresh if possible
- 1 yellow candle
- 1 pencil
- 1 piece of brown paper (paper bags or other recycled materials work best)
- Honey

- Yellow jewelry (optional)
- Yellow fruits (optional, depending on the season)

Instructions:

1. Set the yellow candle in front of the symbol of Oshun on your altar and light it.
2. Close your eyes, relax, and focus on your intention. First, recite it in your mind a couple of times, and if needed, repeat it out loud as well.
3. Place the honey in a bowl beside the candle. Follow up with the yellow fruit and jewelry if you're using them.
4. Open your eyes, place the pumpkin in front of you and carve a circular opening on the top of it.
5. Write your intention down on a piece of paper.
6. Place the paper inside the pumpkin, then take the candle, tip it, and pour the wax on top of the paper.
7. After the pumpkin has been sealed with the wax, repeat your intention.
8. Snuff out the candle.
9. If you have the ability to do so, take the pumpkin to the nearest water source and offer it to Oshun.

If you feel the need to reiterate your intention or need more time to harness Oshun's power, you can relight the candle any time you want during the next five days.

A Prosperity Offering

Even though Oshun can help you get rich, there are other Orishas who can also do this for you. You can choose to invoke the one whose Ashe you need the most according to the area of life you want to prosper in. For example, Olokun may provide material abundance, while Oshun will grant you spiritual wealth. The ritual is based on Oshun's correspondence. If you're working with another Orisha, you'll need to apply the tools associated with the respective deities.

You'll need the following:

- A representation of an Orisha
- 5 oranges

- Honey
- A pinch of ground cinnamon
- 1 large yellow or white candle
- 1 large white plate

Instructions:
1. Set the candle in front of the symbol of the Orisha on your altar and light it.
2. Place the oranges on the plate and drizzle them generously with honey.
3. Recite your intention out loud to ensure Oshun can hear what you need.
4. Sprinkle the cinnamon on top of the oranges.
5. Leave the oranges on the altar beside the candle for five days.
6. When the five days are up, you may dispose of the offering and put away the candle.

As mentioned after the previous ritual, the candle shouldn't be left burning continuously. Snuff it out anytime you leave it to do something else and light it again when you can keep a watch on it. Use fresh oranges so they can stay out safely at room temperature during the five days.

A Prayer for Olokun

The best time to make an offering to Olokun is around the time of the traditional harvest celebrations. However, you can also make this offering at any other date throughout the year if you require her protection or guidance. Doing it in the open air will let Olokun know when she is needed much faster.

You'll need the following:
- A representation of Olokun
- Charcoal
- A piece of white cloth
- Yemaya incense powder
- Cowrie shells

- Fruit, meat, grains, or other offerings of your choice

Instructions:
1. Spread the piece of cloth on your altar and place the representation of Olokun on it in the center of the altar.
2. Pour the charcoal into a small bowl and sprinkle some incense powder over it.
3. Light the powder and place the shells in a basket.
4. Place everything you've prepared for the offering around the basket.
5. Light the candle and recite the following prayer:

    "I honor you, Olokun, the queen of waters.

    I will praise and serve you as long as you keep water on the Earth.

    Let the vast waters be calm, so they bring peace to my soul.

    And I'll respect your water kingdom. Ashé, ashé. "

6. Relax your mind by focusing on the flame of the candle. You can also close your eyes and meditate for a couple of minutes if you find it easier to calm your mind this way.
7. Work on manifesting your intention until the incense burns out, then thank Olokun for the blessing she may bestow on you.

The Yemaya powder can be substituted with another incense powder. Live sacrifices are not recommended in modern practices, so if you offer meat, make sure to use only the cooked part of an animal you have already prepared as a meal for yourself.

A Sour Bath for Overcoming Difficulties

The purpose of this bath is to acknowledge that while your current life experiences may be difficult, good times are still waiting in the wings for you. Immerse yourself in this sour bath made from bitter herbs to see the negativity in and around you and how you can change things to work more in your favor. The seven drops of ammonia represent the seven evil forces in African spirituality.

You'll need the following:
- A cup
- Some tea light candles
- Seven drops of ammonia
- Half a cup of vinegar
- Flowers with red or purple petals
- Fresh or dried bitter herbs, such as dandelion, yarrow, horehound, wormwood, and stinging nettle

Instructions:
1. Just before sunset, start filling up your bathtub with hot water. Adjust the water temperature to how you usually have it.
2. Place the tea light candles around the bathtub's rim and light them.
3. When the water in the tub has reached the desired level, turn off all the other lights in the bathroom.
4. Toss all the ingredients into the water, then enter the tub between two candles.
5. As you immerse yourself in the water and inhale the bitter scent of the herbs, focus on the areas of your life you feel might be harboring negativity.
6. If you require additional guidance, you may also ask Orisha for assistance in chasing away the bitter experiences.
7. Aim to spend seven minutes completely immersed in the water, so make sure to dip your head under from time to time.
8. Once the water starts to grow cold, exit the tub through the same gap between the candles as you got in.
9. Scoop some of your bathwater and other ingredients into the cup before draining your tub.
10. Let yourself dry naturally so the healing effect of the herbs can soak into your skin.
11. Put on dark clothes, and take the cup with the bathwater outside.
12. Stand facing west and hold the cup over your head while saying:

> *"I have now given the Orisha their due. I now ask them to hold onto me. With this water, I cast out all my problems from my head and life. Ashé, ashé!"*

13. Toss out the water from the cup, head back indoors, and spend some time recouping your strength.
14. Drink lots of room-temperature water after the bath to replenish the fluids you have lost while soaking in hot water.

If you want to avoid blocking your drains, place the herbs in a reusable tea bag or cheesecloth. You can include this bath in your regular beauty and healthcare practice. For the best result, apply shea butter or other natural moisturizing agents afterward and avoid using electronics after your bath. Spend your time journaling or meditating instead.

Energizing Bath

This sweet bath is very similar to the previous one, except this one is taken at sunrise to purify and energize you. The ingredients, milk, eggs, and honey, will nourish your body and invigorate your mind anytime you feel the need for some pampering.

You'll need the following:
- A pair of tea light candles
- 3 cups of milk
- Honey
- Powdered cinnamon
- Flowers with all-white petals, such as roses, lilies, white chrysanthemums, and daisies
- Whole nutmeg and powdered nutmeg
- Five different fresh or dried herbs that are invigorating, such as angelica, hyssop, allspice, and comfrey,
- 1 raw egg
- Cocoa butter or shea butter (optional)
- Your favorite perfume
- An empty cup

Instructions:
1. Before sunrise, fill up your bathtub with hot water. Adjust the water temperature.
2. Place the tea light candles around its rim and light them.
3. When the tub is full enough, turn off all the other lights in the bathroom.
4. Crack the egg and toss it in the water. It may start to cook a little bit, but this is normal.
5. Throw on the flowers, herbs, cinnamon, and nutmeg, and pour in the milk and the honey.
6. Add a few drops of your favorite perfume, and gently stir the water to distribute the ingredients evenly.
7. Enter the tub through the gap between two candles.
8. As outlined in the previous ritual, when you enter the water, focus on the good things you already have going on in your life.
9. Consider all the good experiences you may have on that day as well. It's a good idea to express gratitude to the Orishas for these blessings.
10. Aim to spend seven minutes completely immersed in the water, so make sure to dip your head under as well from time to time.
11. Once the water grows cold, get out of the tub through the same gap between the candles you have entered.
12. Scoop some of your bathwater and the ingredients into the cup before draining your tub.
13. Let yourself dry naturally so that the effect of the herbs can soak into your skin.
14. Put on light-colored clothes, and take the cup with the bathwater outside.
15. Stand facing east and hold the cup over your head while saying:

> *"I welcome all the beautiful things in life that are waiting for me on my journey!*

> *As I cast this water where it's needed, I ask the Orishas to bless me with health, love, prosperity, and happiness! Ashé, ashé!"*

16. Toss out the water, head back inside and get ready to welcome the blessings you've invoked.

Once again, place the herbs in a reusable tea bag or cheesecloth to avoid blocking your drains. You can incorporate this bath into your regular beauty and healthcare practice. If you don't have time to meditate, journal, or perform any other self-care routine before heading out for the day, don't worry. Avoiding electronics and stressful situations right after your bath can still help you remain calm and relaxed throughout the day.

Chapter 10: Daily Practices with the Yoruba Calendar

Now that you're familiar with the Yoruba culture and ritual practices, you can put your knowledge into practice. The pivotal point of any culture and spirituality is being able to form a connection between it and your practical life. There are so many Yoruba practices and rituals that can be incorporated into your daily life, and the best way to do that is to first understand the association of each practice and event and then include them into your life one at a time. This chapter will act as a guide to teach you the daily Orisha rituals you can practice and how you can practice African spirituality more often.

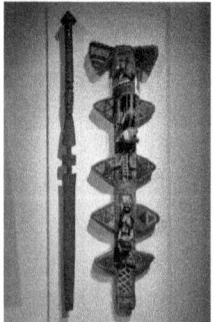

So many Yoruba practices and rituals can be incorporated into your daily life.
Cliff from Arlington, Virginia, USA, CC BY 2.0 <https://creativecommons.org/licenses/by/2.0>, via Wikimedia Commons:
https://commons.wikimedia.org/wiki/File:Staff_and_sheath_for_Orisha_Oko,_Yoruba_peoples,_Oyo_region,_Irawo_village,_Nigeria,_Late_19th_to_early_20th_century,_Staff_iron,_wood_(2923635450).jpg

The Yoruba Calendar

The Yoruba calendar, also commonly referred to as the Kójódá calendar, has been used by the Yoruba people for centuries. Originally, this calendar year began after the last moon of May or before the first moon of June. Traditionally, a Yoruba week is divided into four days dedicated to the Orisha. In contrast, the modern version of this calendar has the week divided into seven days to align with the Gregorian calendar. Whether you want to incorporate Yoruba practices according to the four-day week or the seven-day week is up to you. However, you should be aware that each of these days has its own rites and practices that should be followed.

Days of the Week

For the seven-day week in the Yoruba calendar, each day has a particular meaning associated with it. According to this classification, each day of the week is to be associated with a certain part of your life. So, the rituals and rites you perform on this day should coincide with the specific meaning of the day. Listed below are the practices usually performed each day:

1. **Sunday/Ojó-Àìkú**

Sunday, or Ojo Aiku, is considered the day of rest. According to Yoruba legends, this is the day on which the mother of Esu Odara was buried by Orunmila. On this day, the world's people requested immortality (aiku) from Oludumare. Orunmila, who was a close confidant of Olodumare, refused to appease him. So Oludumare was unable to grant immortality to the people of earth. This is why life has to come to an end. However, it is believed that offering a sacrifice to Oludumare on this day can prevent premature death.

2. **Monday/Ojó-Ajé**

Ojo Aje, or Monday, is the day that the concept of money or wealth was brought to this earth by the Orishas. And so Mondays are associated with all things money-related. As a result, many Yoruba believers consider this day to be the best time to start a business or discuss their finances.

3. Tuesday/Ọjọ́-Ìṣégun

Tuesday is considered to be the day of victory. Many Orisha heroes won great battles and defeated their enemies on this day. So Tuesday is considered to be the time when all evil forces can be overpowered. Many Yoruba people use this day to begin anything that will lead to a better quality of life.

4. Wednesday/Ọjọ́rú

Ojuru, or Wednesday, is the day of confusion or calamities. This is the day that all disruptions, problems, and calamities entered this world. On Wednesdays, most Yoruba people pray against any forms of evil, problems, and confusion.

5. Thursday/Ọjóbọ̀

Ojobo, or Thursday, is the day people's ancestors visit their families. You will notice that most Yoruba festivals begin on this day, making it the week's most important day. Many people also believe that this is when the souls of the departed visit their homes.

6. Friday/Ọjọ́-Ẹtì

This day is considered to be the day of failure. Its meaning is also synonymous with postponement. The Yoruba people believe that whatever is scheduled for a Friday gets postponed or, worse, *fails*. This is why most Yoruba people avoid beginning any business ventures or journeys on this day.

7. Saturday/Ọjọ́-Àbáméta

Saturday, or the day of three suggestions in the Yoruba calendar. This day is considered to be similar to Ojo-Eti or Friday. You shouldn't start anything on this day to avoid three types of negative incidents. It is also advised that you don't bury a person on this day unless they're an elder.

Traditional Yoruba Days of the Week

Originally, the Yoruba calendar consisted of four-day weeks, and each day was dedicated to a particular Orisha. If you want to follow the traditional Yoruba calendar, the following days make up a week.

1. Ojo Ogun

This is the first day of the traditional Yoruba week and is dedicated to Ogun, the god of iron. On this day, you can make numerous food offerings to Ogun. His favorite food items are ekuru, iyan, and ewa. Ogon likes a balanced diet, so your food offerings should be at a balanced level.

2. Ojo Jakuta

The second day of the traditional Yoruba week, Ojo Jakuta, also known as Ojo Sanga, is dedicated to the Orisha of thunder and lightning. The best way to pay tribute to Sanga is to wear red or white clothes, which reflect the Orisha. Food offerings can include guguru, bitter kola, gbegiri soup, amala, and sacrificial ram.

3. Ojo Ose

The third day is dedicated to the worship of the Orisha Nla. On this day, you should wear white to pay tribute to the great deity and also worship Obatala, Iyaami, or Egungun. Food offerings should include beef, but snail sacrifices are also common.

4. Ojo Awo

Also known as the day of the deity, Ojo Awo is dedicated to Ifa, the Oracle. Food offerings should include beef, just like the Orisha Nla. This day can also be used to worship Orunmila, Esu, or Osun.

Yoruba Months

Like the Gregorian calendar, the Yoruba calendar divides the year into 12 months. The only difference is that the Yoruba year starts in June, whereas the Gregorian year starts in January. Each Yoruba month has been dedicated to an Orisha. There are festivals, rituals, and events that take place during each of these months. However, not every month is limited to a single festival and can hold multiple events and rituals that take place every year. Here are some of the many events that are held every year during each of the Yoruba months.

January - Ṣẹrẹ

January, or Sere, is the month dedicated to Obatala, the great Orisha who created the human body. Due to the nature of Obatala's wisdom, rituals related to this Orisha can help solve conflicts, get rid of spiritual wars, help promote peace, tranquility, and calmness, and encourage the balance of peace, good familial relationships, and healing of physical and mental illness.

Luck Ritual. This ritual can be used to bring luck and fortune into your household. For this, you need a white scarf, cocoa butter, cotton grass, white marigold seeds, husk, and plenty of blades of grass. Take each of the ingredients and grind them into a fine powder. Place a leaf on the white cloth or scarf. Place the powdered ingredients on the leaf and set your intention for the ritual. Ask Obatala to charge the magic dust with luck and fortune and leave it for eight days. After this, clean yourself with this dust, and blow it out of the house.

February - Èrèlé

February or Erele is dedicated to Olokun, the Orisha of Okun, or the ocean. He was considered the guardian of souls lost at sea, the controller of deep seas and oceans, and the patron of sailors. Olokun is considered the harbinger of health, wealth, and other material things. One of the most common ritual substances associated with Olokun is the Akh'Olokun or Olokun pots.

The ritual itself consists of a bath for purifying the souls of worshippers. A pot should be filled with fresh river water and some river leaves. The Orisha Olokun should then be asked to charge the water to purify whoever it touches. Finally, the water should be poured over your head. The pot itself needs to have imagery of a python, a ram, and a cock, which are all sacrificial animals for this particular Orisha.

March - Ẹrẹ̀nà

Erena, or the month of March, is associated with multiple Orishas and festivals. First, the annual rites of passage for men are celebrated during this month. Secondly, it is dedicated to Oduduwa, the Orisha of Earth, also known as the father of the Yoruba people, and secondly, to Osoosi, the Orisha of hunting and adventure. The annual rites of passage for men consist of a series of tests and rituals boys undergo. If they succeed in completing these tests, they will have passed the rites of passage and be considered men instead of boys.

April - Igbe

This month begins with the onset of the rainy season. It is dedicated to Ogun, the Orisha of metalworking, crafts, and engineering. He was considered to be the custodian of truth and justice. Oshun, the Orisha of fertility and pregnancies, also has a part in the month of April. Usually, the Oshun festival is the most popular event during this month. The festivities start with a lamp-lighting ceremony followed by a visit to the Arugba shrine. After that, the procession is led to the sacred grove where thousands of people get cleansed from the water. There are also brilliant pageants and parties thrown for the goddess of love and springs.

May - Èbìbì

May has been dedicated to Egungun, which signifies the ancestors' commemoration, especially the community's founders, and is celebrated by the Egungun festival. The annual masquerade festival pays tribute to the ancestral spirits through a series of masked dances, depending on the history of the local ancestors. For instance, if your region's ancestors were famous warriors, then the Egungun festival dances should be chaotic and wild, reflecting the nature of the ancestral spirits. Exquisite Egungun costumes are designed to cover your whole body, and the ancestral spirit is considered to be concealed inside the cloth. The cloth itself acts as an offering to the spirits.

June - Òkúdù

Okudu (or June) is the month the new year begins in the Yoruba calendar. Dedicated to Shopona and Osanyin, the Orishas of disease and healing, respectively, both of these Orishas are connected together because where there's a disease, there's healing. This month also celebrates the annual rites of passage of women. And finally, dedicated to Yemoja, who is considered the mother of Orisha.

It is said that Oduduwa gave birth to Yemojaa (water) and Aganju (land) from marriage with Obatala. She then gave birth to many other Orisha and is considered the Orisha of water, fertility, and women. The Yemoja-Moremi festival is celebrated this month. Throughout the celebrations, many pageants and fertility dances take place to pay tribute to the mother goddess of Yoruba. The rites of passage for girls also occur during this time, similar to the masculine rites.

July - Agẹmọ

The month of July is dedicated to Orunmila, who is associated with divination and is considered the founder of the Ifa sciences. This is the month of mass Yoruba gatherings for festivals and rituals. Oko, the Orisha of agriculture, is also paid tribute to during July. This time is considered perfect for harvesting the new yam crop. Agemo is also dedicated to Esu-Elegba, the great communicator and messenger of Olodumare. Finally, the Orisha of energy, Sango, is also worshiped this month. The Sango festival takes place during the last week of July. The festivities pay tribute to the Alaafin of Oyo, who later became the god of thunder and lightning.

August - Ògún

The famous Osun-Osogbo festival takes place in August. This month is dedicated to Osun, the Orisha of fertility and female essence. At the same time, the month of Ogun is also dedicated to Ogun, the Orisha of metals, technology, and engineering. The fact that there are two months in the Yoruba calendar paying tribute to Ogun reflects the esteem of this Orisha in Yoruba culture. August also consists of the annual Obatala festival, where many plays and stately dances are performed to show respect for the patron god of Yoruba culture.

September - Ọwẹ́wẹ̀ or Owewe

September or Owewe is considered a month of blessings and celebrations. During this month, many new yam festivals are celebrated, and the Yoruba culture in its entirety is celebrated.

October - Ọ̀wàrà or Ọ̀wààrà

Owara translates to rain and refers to the rainy season that begins during October. This month is thus dedicated to the Orisha of rivers, Oya. He was also considered the guardian of the gateway between the physical and spiritual realms. This month is the onset of the dry season. It is also dedicated to Sigidi, the Orisha of unsettled spirits that have left the physical realm but are forbidden to enter Orun-Rere or heaven. Moreover, King's day is also celebrated during the first week of October to honor the king's birthday. A grand series of processions, feasts, and banquets are observed during these festivities.

November - Bélú

November is not considered a particularly special month. But it can still be considered spiritually enhancing. Several Yoruba rites and rituals are not associated with any particular month or day that can take place during this time.

December - Ọ̀pẹ

December marks the onset of the Hammayan season and is dedicated to Obaluaye, the Orisha of healing and disease. Festivities during this season include tributes paid to Obalauye through sacrifices and offerings. Sacred dances and processions are also held to worship the Orisha of this month.

There are countless Yoruba rituals, festivals, and events to show your devotion to your spirituality. However, until you understand the timing of each festival and rite of passage, you cannot perform them successfully. Once you're aware of each Yoruba festival's occurrence throughout the year, you can successfully add many rituals and rites into your daily life, and better follow your culture.

Extra: Orisha Glossary

- **Aganju:** Aganju is considered the Yoruba spirit of volcanoes. He embodies the essence of fire and is considered one of the fathers of nature. This Orisha is represented by the sun and is tasked with assisting humans in reaching their destinies. He transforms the fire within into passion or empowerment.
- **Agayu:** The alternative name of Aganju Orisha.
- **Aje:** Also known as the other mothers, Aje are wise women having extraordinary powers who can make people both fear and revere them.
- **Ajé Saluga:** The Yoruba wealth god, Ajé Saluga, Aje Shaluga, or Aye Shaluga, is considered to be extremely generous. He showers his followers with riches, as he's one of the richest Orishas.
- **Babalú Ayé:** The Yoruba healer god, Babalú Ayé goes by many names, including Babalu Aye, Babaluaiye, Babaluaye, or Obaluaye. He is a hardworking Orisha who helps treat infections, epidemics, and nasty infestations.
- **Bayani:** The goddess of hats, sister of Shango, and bearer of knowledge that the ceremonial headpiece encrusted with shells provides. She is also known by Babayanmi, Banyani, Bayanni, Bayoni, and Bayonni.

- **Chango:** Also known as Shango, or Xango, the god of storms, is a popular deity in Yoruba culture. He is also considered to be the god of war. Originally, he was a famous warrior hero of the Yoruba people and ascended to be an Orisha. He is the brother of Ogun, who he doesn't get along with, and the lover of Oya.
- **Dada:** The abundance god of Yoruba people, Dada, more commonly referred to as Dada Segbo, produces organic natural goods. Thus, he is also believed to assist in the birth of children.
- **Eda:** The alternative namesake of Dada Sagbo, god of natural produce.
- **Egungun-Oya:** The goddess of divination is in charge of fortune-telling and prophecy readings. She can predict people's future, as well as their powers.
- **Eleggua:** Eleggua, Èṣù-Ẹlẹ́gbára or Elegua, is the Yoruba trickster god, also considered the guardian of the crossroads of life. Therefore, he is also the Orisha of crossroads, opportunities, and beginnings. He is also the messenger for other Orisha, particularly Olorun. He's usually associated with mischief, trickery, and mayhem.
- **Elusu:** Also commonly known as Olokun-Su, or the wife of Olokun, the Orisha of the sea. Elusu is as benevolent as she is beautiful. She represents the many creatures of the sea, especially fish. She is mostly associated with water.
- **Eshu:** Another Yoruba trickster god, Eshu or Esu, is tremendously popular and known by everyone. He's considered the god of instant messaging, communication, and opportunity and is said to direct people on the road of life at the crossroads of fortune. He is associated with trickery and mischief, fortune, and luck.
- **Hare:** Yet another trickster god associated with mischief and mayhem. His most common form is a twitchy-nosed rabbit or hare, hence the name.

- **Jakuta:** A Yoruba thunderstorm god, also known as the thrower of light. While many confuse Jakuta with Shango, they are two separate Orisha deities. Jakuta was present long before Shango was declared an Orisha. He is also associated with lightning.
- **Morimi:** A Yoruba fire goddess, Morimi is known as the goddess of bush burning. Associated mainly with fire, Morimi is said to have quite a temper, as all fire-associated Orishas do.
- **Obatalá:** The creator of the human race and the Yoruba god of purity, Obatala goes by many names, including Obàtálá, Orisha-Popo, Olufon, Orisanla, Orisala Orisha-Nla, Oshanla, and Orishala. Considered one of the high-ranking Orishas, Obatala was tasked with creating the Earth by his father, Olorun. While he's mainly associated with purity, other roles falling under his jurisdiction include fortune, childbirth, and fertility. Obatala is married to Yemaya.
- **Ochosi:** A Yoruba hunting god, Ochosi, Ocshosi, Oxósse, or Oxossi, is among the most influential and skilled Orishas. He is great at hunting his prey, no matter how elusive. He is also commonly associated with justice and has a bow and arrow to help with the task.
- **Odudua:** One of the most renowned Orishas, Odudua goes by many names, including Odudu, Odua, and Oduwa. She is the Yoruba earth goddess, with skin the darkest shade of ebony. Tales of her beauty are legendary in Yoruba mythology. She looks after children and women, promoting love and laughter among humans. She is one of the highest-ranking primordial Orishas and the sister of Olomare. Together, both siblings form an earth-sky bond. She is associated with the essence of life and is married to Obatala.
- **Odùduwà:** Oduduwa is the hero god of the Yoruba people. He is the one who showed up for the creation of the earth after his brother, Obatala, failed to complete it. As a reward, Oduduwa was given the title of the Orisha of Earth. He later went down to rule over the Yoruba people and was their first King. Oduduwa and Odudua are often confused with being

the same deity but are, in fact, two different entities.

- **Ogun:** The Yoruba weaponry god, Ogun had many titles, including the Orisha of metalwork, engineering, and iron. Although he is one of the hunting Orishas, he specializes in weapon creation using iron and other metals. He is also often associated with justice and oaths.
- **Oko:** The Yoruba agriculture god, Oko is considered to be the Orisha of farming. He is the son of Yemaya and was sent to the earth to encourage the bountiful production of goods. He is thus associated with fertile farming.
- **Olodumare:** The supreme Orisha and Yoruba god, Olodumare or Olorun, is one of the primordial deities who started it all. He is considered to be the sky god of peace, justice, and the Yoruba way. He is associated with everything supreme.
- **Olokun:** Another highly popular Orisha, the Yoruba god of the sea and the husband of Elusu, Olokun is associated with the ocean, rivers, and the sea. He is quick to anger and easily agitated. He was often at odds with Obatala and other Orishas.
- **Onile:** The Orisha of metalwork, Onile is often confused for Ogun; however, she is associated with soft metalwork. So, while Ogun is associated mainly with iron and other hard metals, Onile is associated with soft metals like aluminum and blacksmithing.
- **Orunmila:** The Yoruba god of wisdom and divinity, Orunmila is also very famous in Yoruba mythology. He is one of the most useful spirits of knowledge.
- **Osanyin:** The Yoruba god of herbs, Osanyin is another popular Orisha. He's mainly associated with medicinal herbs, plants, and vegetation. In contrast to agriculture Orishas, Osanyin is connected to the herbs and medicinal purposes of plants instead of being responsible for growing them. He has knowledge of all the herbs.

- **Oshe:** A safety staff used by storm gods. This staff is associated with the thunder god Shango, who is the calmest thunder Orishas of them all.
- **Oshun:** The Yoruba goddess of love, Oshun (or Osun) is associated with love, sensuality, and creativity. She is also considered to be the protective Orisha of the river Oshun. She blesses all kinds of intimacy.
- **Oshunmare:** Known as the Yoruba rainbow spirit, Oshunmare is a serpent Orisha who is said to be a colorful serpent that makes up the rainbow.
- **Oya:** The Yoruba goddess of practically everything, Oya is a multitasking Orisha mainly tasked with the duty of protecting the River Niger. She is also associated with funerals, weather, and different diseases.
- **Shapona:** He is the scarlet-robed Orisha of smallpox and is definitely not the most popular Orisha, though he is much feared. He's mainly associated with sickness and diseases but also checks the correct observance of rituals.
- **Yansan:** The Yoruba wind goddess, Yansan, is the most mysterious Orisha among them all. Some people say that this is Oya in disguise. She is associated with the wind.
- **Yemaya:** The Yoruba goddess of Childbirth, Yemaya is a famous female Orisha who is not just powerful but also sensuous. She is associated with water, and her personality is fluid, just like water. She is also considered to be the moon goddess and is Obatala's wife. She also goes by the names Iamanjie, Yemayah, Yemanja, Yembo, Yemonja, Yemoja, and Yemowo.

Conclusion

African spirituality is based on beliefs that reflect a strong respect for the divine and the souls of the departed. Ancestral souls are often given the same amount of significance as divinities. The various traditional customs in the different beliefs create a highly diverse set of practices that evolved through history and now span across multiple continents. Several other religious systems have influenced African spiritual practices.

Yet no matter how different their cultural background may be, the traditional African beliefs of Yoruba, Santeria, Voodoo, and Hoodoo all have similar elements. One aspect all these religions have is the existence of a Supreme god, also called Olodumare or Olorun. His contribution to the creation of life on Earth makes several appearances in the respective practices, as does the existence of the Orishas, the divine souls responsible for communication between the Supreme god and people. The Supreme god's energy flows through their Orishas, which is how they carry the messages that otherwise wouldn't reach their destination.

Apart from their role as messengers, the Orishas can also help people on their spiritual journey using their Ashe. This is a unique form of energy that can fend off misfortune and subdue malicious spirits. Practitioners of various African spiritual arts may call upon it when they need protection, guidance, or help with healing. Instead of the Orishas, some African belief systems have the Loa as their divine messengers. In fact, one of the most prominent roles of Loas is guiding souls between the world and helping them move on to different lives after passing.

The Orishas are classified as white, or cool-tempered, and dark, or hot-tempered Orishas. White Orishas are known for having calming and gentle natures. They are usually contacted when one needs help with emotional trauma. Red and black Orishas have more passionate natures and can provide protection. All Orishas have their preferred Ebo (offering) and favorite colors to be used during spells, rituals, and ceremonies. The dark Orishas are particularly sensitive to these objects and often consider certain offerings taboo. Before asking for their assistance, you must be sure they will be properly pleased. Otherwise, you risk angering them.

As you may have surmised, another common factor of African religions is their spiritual nature. The unique worldview of African spirituality revolves around the soul's journey through birth, death, and rebirth. And with each reincarnation, the soul is elevated to a higher level until it becomes one with the Supreme God. One of the most common ways spirituality is practiced in these religions is by building an altar. This is a dedicated space to honor the deities, your ancestors, and your spiritual journey. While having an altar to develop your practice is unnecessary, it can be helpful for beginners who are just learning how to use their intuition. Whether making Voodoo dolls, gris-gris, mojo bags, enacting spells, or rituals, doing a cleansing ceremony, or any other African magical practice, your most important tool will be your intuition. As an extension of your spiritual self, your gut will tell you the best way to approach each practice. You can also follow the Yoruba calendar. This is a great tool for incorporating African spirituality into your day-to-day life. It teaches you how to honor each Orisha, the best time to connect with your ancestors, and much more.

Here's another book by Silvia Hill that you might like

Free Bonus from Silvia Hill available for limited time

Hi Spirituality Lovers!

My name is Silvia Hill, and first off, I want to THANK YOU for reading my book.

Now you have a chance to join my exclusive spirituality email list so you can get the ebooks below for free as well as the potential to get more spirituality ebooks for free! Simply click the link below to join.

P.S. Remember that it's 100% free to join the list.

~~$27~~ FREE BONUSES

9 Types of Spirit Guides and How to Connect to Them

How to Develop Your Intuition: 7 Secrets for Psychic Development and Tarot Reading

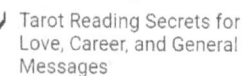
Tarot Reading Secrets for Love, Career, and General Messages

Access your free bonuses here
https://livetolearn.lpages.co/african-spirituality-paperback/

References

Barrett, O. (2022, January 23). Voodoo: The revolutionary roots of the most misunderstood religion. TheCollector.
https://www.thecollector.com/voodoo-history-misunderstood-religion/

Beyer, C. (2010, February 1). An introduction to the basic beliefs of the Vodou (Voodoo) religion. Learn Religions.
https://www.learnreligions.com/vodou-an-introduction-for-beginners-95712

Bjorling, J. (2013). Reincarnation: A Bibliography. Routledge.
https://www.yogapedia.com/definition/5833/reincarnation

Chiorazzi, A. (2015, October 6). The spirituality of Africa. Harvard Gazette.
https://news.harvard.edu/gazette/story/2015/10/the-spirituality-of-africa/

Coles, D. (2020, October 21). An introduction to hoodoo. Cosmopolitan.
https://www.cosmopolitan.com/lifestyle/a34115081/hoodoo-vs-voodoo-facts-history/

Dev, B. (2016, February 4). Eight interesting facts about the Yoruba people. Bashiri. https://bashiri.com.au/eight-interesting-facts-yoruba-people/

Ekore, R. I., & Lanre-Abass, B. (2016). African cultural concept of death and the idea of advance care directives. Indian Journal of Palliative Care, 22(4), 369–372. https://doi.org/10.4103/0973-1075.191741

Knoetze, J. J. (2019). African spiritual phenomena and the probable influence on African families. In Die Skriflig/In Luce Verbi, 53(4), 1–8.
https://doi.org/10.4102/ids.v53i4.2505

Obamwonyi, H. (2016, June 18). Life after death according to several African traditions. SwaliAfrica Magazine; SwaliAfrica.
http://blog.swaliafrica.com/life-after-death-according-to-several-african-traditions/

Singh, C., & Bhagwan, R. (2020). African spirituality: Unearthing beliefs and practices for the helping professions. Social Work, 56(4), 403–415. https://doi.org/10.15270/56-4-882

The ancient roots of Yoruba. (2005, September 30). Tampa Bay Times. https://www.tampabay.com/archive/1997/01/07/the-ancient-roots-of-yoruba/

The Editors of Encyclopedia Britannica. (2022). reincarnation. In Encyclopedia Britannica.

The Santeria religion, a story. (2009, September 8). African American Registry. https://aaregistry.org/story/from-africa-to-the-americas-santeria/

What is Santeria? (n.d.). AboutSanteria. http://www.aboutsanteria.com/what-is-santeria.html

Wigington, P. (2011, November 15). What is the Santeria religion? Learn Religions. http://learnreligions.com/about-santeria-traditions-2562543

Wigington, P. (2019, November 29). Yoruba religion: History and beliefs. Learn Religions. https://www.learnreligions.com/yoruba-religion-4777660

Yoruba. (n.d.). Everyculture.com. https://www.everyculture.com/wc/Mauritania-to-Nigeria/Yoruba.html

Abisoye. (2021, August 11). Olodumare, the god with no images, shrines. Plus TV Africa. https://plustvafrica.com/olodumare-the-god-with-no-images-shrines/

Baggini, J. (2006, March 27). Why do we have creation myths? The Guardian. https://amp.theguardian.com/theguardian/2006/mar/28/features11.g21

Creation Myth. (n.d.). Nau.edu. https://www2.nau.edu/~gaud/bio301/content/crtm.htm

LibGuides: African traditional religions textbook: Ifa: Chapter 4. Olodumare is a gracious creator. (2021). https://research.auctr.edu/Ifa/Chap4Intro

Olodumare –. (n.d.). Eneke The Bird. https://enekethebird.wordpress.com/tag/olodumare/

OLODUMARE - the Yoruba Religious concepts. (n.d.). Google.com. https://sites.google.com/site/theyorubareligiousconcepts/olodumare

Olodumare, Olorun and Olofin: The names of God. (2022, February 7). Oshaeifa.com. https://en.oshaeifa.com/orisha/olodumare-olorun-olofin/

Olujobi, H. (2016, September 24). The lies of their forefathers: Yoruba myth of creation. Linkedin.com. https://www.linkedin.com/pulse/lies-forefathers-yoruba-myth-creation-hezekiah-olujobi/

Rodríguez, C. (2020, August 11). Who are Olofin Olorun and Olodumare? Ashé pa mi Cuba. https://ashepamicuba.com/en/quienes-son-olofin-olorun-y-olodumare/

Yoruba creation myth. (n.d.). Gateway-africa.com. https://www.gateway-africa.com/stories/Yoruba_Creation_Myth.html

Beyer, C. (2012, June 11). The Orishas. Learn Religions. https://www.learnreligions.com/who-are-the-orishas-95922

Brandon, G. (2018). orisha. In Encyclopedia Britannica.

Burton, N. (2020, July 31). How some Black Americans are finding solace in African spirituality. Vox. https://www.vox.com/2020/7/31/21346686/orisha-yoruba-african-spirituality-covid

Fields, K. (2020, January 18). The Seven African Powers for beginners (African spirituality & magic). Otherworldly Oracle; FIELDS CREATIVE CONSULTING. https://otherworldlyoracle.com/seven-african-powers/

Mark, J. J. (2021). Orisha. World History Encyclopedia. https://www.worldhistory.org/Orisha/

Murphy, J. M. (2022). Santería. In Encyclopedia Britannica.

Nigeria, G. (2019, August 11). The 5 most influential orishas. The Guardian Nigeria News - Nigeria and World News; Guardian Nigeria. https://guardian.ng/life/the-5-most-influential-orishas/

demo. (2016, September 20). Who are the Orishas? DJONIBA Dance Center. https://www.djoniba.com/who-are-the-orishas/

Konkwo, R. (2022, September 21). Yoruba gods and goddesses: their history explained in detail. Legit.Ng - Nigeria News; Legit.ng. https://www.legit.ng/1175618-yoruba-gods-goddesses.html

Mark, J. J. (2021). Orisha. World History Encyclopedia. https://www.worldhistory.org/Orisha/

Ogbodo, I. (2022, March 17). Yoruba mythology: The orishas of the Yoruba religion. African History Collections. https://medium.com/african-history-collections/yoruba-mythology-the-orishas-of-the-yoruba-religion-f411c3db389d

Orisha orunmila. (n.d.). Themythdetective.com. https://themythdetective.com/index.php/orisha-orunmila/

Ost, B. (2021). LibGuides: African traditional religions textbook: Ifa: Chapter 1. Orientation and overview. https://research.auctr.edu/Ifa/Chap1Intro

Wigington, P. (2019, November 29). Yoruba religion: History and beliefs. Learn Religions. https://www.learnreligions.com/yoruba-religion-4777660

Mark, J. J. (2021). Orisha. World History Encyclopedia. https://www.worldhistory.org/Orisha/

www.ingramcontent.com/pod-product-compliance
Lightning Source LLC
Chambersburg PA
CBHW070337010526
44107CB00004B/535